simplify
your time

simplify
your time

stop running & start living!

MARCIA RAMSLAND,
THE ORGANIZING PRO

THOMAS NELSON
Since 1798

NASHVILLE DALLAS MEXICO CITY RIO DE JANEIRO BEIJING

Published in Nashville, Tennessee, by Thomas Nelson. Thomas Nelson is a trademark of Thomas Nelson, Inc.

Published in association with the literary agency Alive Communications Inc., 7680 Goddard Street, Suite 200, Colorado Springs, CO 80920, www.alivecommunications.com.

Thomas Nelson, Inc., titles may be purchased in bulk for educational, business, fund-raising, or sales promotional use. For information, please e-mail SpecialMarkets@ThomasNelson.com.

The names and identities of clients mentioned have been changed or concealed in composites to protect their privacy. For those who granted permission to print their names, details about their lives appear as they happened.

Editors: Karen O'Connor and Jennifer Stair
Acquisitions Editor: Debbie Wickwire
Cover Design: Terra Peterson at www.brandnavigation.com
Interior Design: Stacy Clark

Library of Congress Cataloging-in-Publication Data

Ramsland, Marcia.
    Simplify your time : stop running and start living! / Marcia Ramsland.
      p. cm.
    ISBN: 978-0-8499-1458-4
    1. Home economics. 2. Time management. I. Title.
    TX147.R368 2006
    640—dc22

2006012958

Printed in the United States of America

08 09 10 RRD 9 8 7

Praise for *Simplify Your Time*

"Marcia Ramsland's easy-to-read book will motivate you to create the time you need to live the life you want. With over twenty years of experience as a professional organizer, her eye-opening, time-saving tools and tips will give you the insight to *Simplify Your Time* and more!"

BARRY J. IZSAK
President, National Association of Professional Organizers

"Time is all we have. Here's a way to maximize it and get great results."

MARK VICTOR HANSEN
Co-creator, #1 *New York Times* Best-selling series *Chicken Soup for the Soul* ®
Co-author, *Cracking the Millionaire Code* and *The One Minute Millionaire*

"No one ever said life is easy, but my friend and colleague Marcia Ramsland really makes it simple. Follow her advice and discover years of free time. I did!"

DR. DENIS WAITLEY
Author, *Timing is Everything*

"Who couldn't use more time? Marcia's book is like being given the gift of time! Thanks Marcia, I hope millions of men and women also get the gift of your book!"

PAM FARREL
Speaker and Author, *10 Best Decisions a Woman Can Make*

"I thought I knew a lot about time management until I read *Simplify Your Time*. Marcia Ramsland has challenged me to get off 'the gerbil wheel of life' and to start developing routines and systems that will make me more effective in my role as a wife, mother, and business owner. Every page is packed with stress-reducing and time-saving habits, tools, skills, and strategies that will make me more productive when I'm working, and free of guilt when I'm not. If you need more hours in your day, read this noteworthy book!"

CAROL KENT
Speaker and Author, *Becoming a Woman of Influence*

"Help! I want off the merry-go-round! My head is spinning, I'm going too fast, I'm not sure I can keep up!" If that's your cry, Marcia's book can help you live a more balanced life. You will find her short chapters very easy and quick to digest. A plus feature to the book is her 101 Time Saving Tips. A must-read for those who want to make sense of the maze of life."

EMILIE BARNES
Speaker, Author, and Founder of *More Hours in My Day*

"I loved *Simplify Your Life*, Marcia's first book. I was so impressed that I wrote her from my organized desk, 'Now I'm ready for the next book.' And here it is! Now we have time to get things done and live the life we want."

JOANNE ROLLER, C.P.C.
Senior Recruiting Consultant

"After reading Marcia's suggestions, I am motivated to manage my time. I never realized how much time we really *do* have control over."

ANN LARSON
Tax Accountant and Author

"So much to do with so little time, or so I once thought! As a homemaker, mom, and with a part-time business at home, it's overwhelming to have a full calendar and a huge pile of projects that never seem to get done. Marcia has changed all that with *Simplify Your Time*, teaching us to break it down into smaller opportunities to be accomplished so we are not facing a mountain of frustration—very needed."

TINA DEARMONT
Homemaker and Former Executive Assistant

This book is dedicated . . .

to you, my busy friend,
in search of more time and a simpler lifestyle,

to my clients, who insist I teach them how to better manage their time
after I organize their offices and homes,

to Larry Nelson, a favorite client and friend, whose legacy reminds
me that you can live a full life of friends, productivity, and purpose
even if it is shortened by tragedy at age forty-seven,

and to my mother, Dorothy Rasmussen, age eighty-nine,
who outlived all our relatives
and reminds me that life can be satisfying at
every age and stage.

Life is a gift. Live it to its fullest by using your time well.

Contents

A Word from the Author   xi

Day 1   Today *Is* the Time of Your Life   1

Week 1
Time-Saving Habits to Simplify Your Daily Life

Day 2   Punch Up Your Punctuality   9
Day 3   Save Time with Two-Minute Pickups   15
Day 4   Get Off Your Computer and On with Your Life   21
Day 5   Power Through Your Paperwork   27
Day 6   Clean Up the Clutter   33
Day 7   Plan Tomorrow the Night Before   40
Day 8   Change a Habit, Change Your Life   44

Week 2
Time-Saving Tools to Simplify Managing Your Time

Day 9   Capture More Time by Controlling Your Calendar   53
Day 10   Fine-Tune Your To-Do List   59
Day 11   Pursue a Personal Project List   65
Day 12   Put It All Together in a Planner System   71
Day 13   Practice the Power of Prioritizing   77
Day 14   Spruce Up Your Support Tools   83
Day 15   Create Weekly Time-Saving Routines   89

Week 3
Time-Saving Skills to Simplify Your Lifestyle

Day 16	Take Time for Relationships	99
Day 17	Simply Find More Personal Time	104
Day 18	Discover Your Rhythm for Each Week	110
Day 19	Master the Secrets of Successful Multitasking	117
Day 20	Overcome When You're Overwhelmed	123
Day 21	Learn to Delegate and Say No	129
Day 22	Take Some Downtime Each Day	135

Week 4
Time-Saving Strategies to Simplify Your Future

Day 23	Jump-Start Your Dreams with a Five-Year Calendar	143
Day 24	Upgrade Your PQ (Project Quotient)	151
Day 25	Do Less to Accomplish More	157
Day 26	Go for Goals That Simplify Your Life	164
Day 27	Ensure Your Future with a Strong Family Network	171
Day 28	Stop Time to Handle a Life Crisis	177
Day 29	Make Today the Best Day of Your Life	184
Day 30	Start Living—Today!	191
Time Management Resources		197
About the Author		199

A Word from the Author

Since you picked up this book, you are probably very busy and looking for more time in your life. (Or you really liked the cover.)

I told my publisher that people who need more time don't have time to read a book; they need answers right now! So after some brainstorming, we agreed that if we organized the book in short, digestible chapters that could be easily applied, it would be *invaluable*. That's what you have in your hands. Thirty short, practical chapters that will give you everything you need to learn the nuances of simplifying your time. You can read a chapter each day, or you can read an entire section in one sitting. The important thing is that you immediately start to apply what you are reading and build on those skills day after day.

When you think about it, everything happens in time: work projects, social events, travel and hobbies, crises and celebrations. We can simplify our time by evaluating our lives, learning new skills, and being intentional about where our time is going.

Studies have shown we have more than two hundred inputs a day—e-mail, mail, thoughts, decisions, memos, phone calls, and on and on the list goes. But our short-term memory only holds seven items at a time. This explains why we often feel overloaded. To clear your mind and simplify your time, you need to know the best habits, tools, shortcuts, and strategies of time management. And I promise to make this book interesting by including client and personal stories to illustrate just how you can apply them.

Be ready to learn and to be entertained. Consider me your "time coach" as we warm up on the racetrack of life. Let this be your personal time management guide to help you relieve stress, find time for yourself, and create a lifestyle that supports you to get more done in less time.

Simplify Your Time: Stop Running and Start Living! is the practical application of the time management books you may have read and loved. From now on you'll know how to save time, spend time, capture time, and multiply your time to simplify your life. Let's get started!

Warmly,
Marcia Ramsland
The Organizing Pro

Day 1

Today *Is* the Time
of Your Life

Being rich is having money;
being wealthy is having time.

—Margaret Bonnano

"Hi, honey. All 168 boxes are packed and ready to go." I held the phone in one hand and a well worn to-do list in the other as I sank into a chair. I was relieved to tell my husband that all of our belongings and I would soon join him. David was already in California while I was closing things out at our home in upstate New York after our decision to move across the country for his new job. Our three teens would join us later that week.

As we talked, I suddenly noticed a gaping hole with only the prongs standing upright on my engagement ring. I gasped and almost dropped the phone. "Oh no! My diamond is missing! David, you won't believe it. It's gone!" At that moment, a million thoughts raced through my mind. Where did I lose it? The movers had just spent two days packing boxes which were ready to be picked up and delivered. I could just picture our three teenagers unpacking the boxes at the other end and me distraught with agony, scolding them, "Be careful. My diamond could be in there."

I knew I didn't want to add any more tension than we already felt. So I took a deep breath and spoke to David in a calm voice. "OK. What do I do now? Was it insured?"

"No," David said, "but don't worry; just come. Everything is great here in California."

"What?! It's not insured?" I didn't know whether to scream or cry. This was no ordinary gem. My husband had picked out the diamond especially for me when he was a college student traveling through Europe with his family.

Was That My Only Diamond?

That night I went to dinner with friends and their two sons, and I told them my dilemma. "We'll go back and find it," offered one of the boys. Their parents were eager to come too. However, there was one obstacle—no lights in the house. "No problem, we'll bring flashlights," they volunteered.

After dinner, the five of us went back to our empty home. In the darkness, we focused our flashlights on every step we took. "Where were you today?" my friend asked.

I remembered going up the attic steps, so we decided to start there. Carefully, we unfolded the stairs from the ceiling and creaked up one step at a time. Then down the stairs. Next we explored the bedroom . . . the family room . . . the kitchen . . . the living room. As we walked carefully through the last room, I began to lose hope of ever seeing my diamond again.

I paused to regain my thoughts and asked of no one in particular, "Now what would this diamond look like?" I glanced down at the carpet tweeds. "It would look like this," I said as I spied something shiny like a piece of plastic wrap. When I picked it up, it held its shape. It was my diamond!

There it was—just sitting at the foot of the attic folding stairs. All five of

> **Time-Saving Tip #1**
>
> If I have a clear mental picture of what I'm looking for, I can take steps to find it.

us had been up and down that stairway looking for it, yet we missed it. Thankfully, I now had a second chance to appreciate my treasure.

Time Management Lessons from My Diamond Hunt

I learned some lessons from that emotion-packed diamond hunt that relate to our topic of simplifying time:

LESSON #1: WHAT I DIDN'T KNOW WAS COSTLY. As a starry-eyed fiancée, I must have missed the instructions to regularly check the prongs holding the diamond. Regular maintenance would have saved me from a crisis at a critical moment in life.

In time management, there are some basic rules, tools, and skills you need to keep your life running smoothly too. Don't wait for a crisis to realize you missed some important steps. You'll learn them in this book.

> **Time-Saving Tip #2**
>
> Remember, time is on your side if you use it well. But it works against you if you bite off more than you can chew.

LESSON #2: I TOOK IT FOR GRANTED. I was wearing my diamond every day but not really seeing it. I liked knowing it was there, but I didn't realize I needed to take better care of it.

Something similar can happen with time. We use time every day, but we don't realize it can get away from us if we don't manage it well.

LESSON #3: WHEN I KNEW WHAT I WAS LOOKING FOR, I FOUND IT. I thought I knew what my diamond would look like, but I missed it several times. Until I focused on the gem's qualities of size, shape, and color, it remained lost to me.

To simplify your time, you need a clear picture of what you want to find, such as an hour a day to rest or read, an evening a week to meet with friends, or a weekend a month to focus on a hobby or to take a trip. Without attention to your personal goals, you'll never "find" the time to do these things.

It takes insight and new perspective to see what we have missed. In this book, I will give you both.

Your Time Is Simple; Your Life Is Not

If practice makes perfect, then we should be awesome time managers! After all, we have been using time every day of our lives. So why aren't we experts at using our time? Because life happens to us. Because we get fuzzy and unfocused. Because we get tired of the "have-tos" and prefer the "want-tos" but get trapped in the "never-get-around-tos." And before we realize it, we run out of time.

When you need more time, where do you go to get it? There are no ATMs or banks for time deposits or withdrawals. But there is something you can do: redistribute your commitments and spend time where you want to. You have 24 hours a day, 168 hours per week, and 8,736 hours per year. They contain all the time you need to achieve the hopes and dreams you were created for—one day at a time.

> **Time-Saving Tip #3**
>
> You can add time to your life by deleting an activity that is unproductive. But you multiply your time when you add an activity that energizes you.

Simplify Your Time—How?

To simplify your time, you need to look at the key strategies used by successful time managers, people much like you. These strategies comprise four main categories, and I've chosen one focus per week. Under each category, we'll look at one key skill each day that you can immediately put into practice to simplify your time.

Each week, you'll save enough time to enjoy some extra downtime—whether for work, family, or fun. By the end of our thirty-day journey, you'll be ready to plan future goals and sail right through them. Here's the agenda ahead:

WEEK 1: PRACTICAL TIME-SAVING HABITS. From making your bed to handling your paperwork, good habits done quickly will save you lots of time and help your day run smoothly.

WEEK 2: PRACTICAL TIME-SAVING TOOLS. With the right tools, you'll be able to organize, simplify, maintain your time, and minimize stress as you respond to myriad daily challenges.

WEEK 3: PRACTICAL TIME-SAVING SKILLS. Once you have implemented time-saving habits and time tools, you'll want to learn the skills to "break the rules" and solve problems that arise.

WEEK 4: PRACTICAL TIME-SAVING STRATEGIES. Once your everyday life is working, you'll have time to look ahead and plan for future seasons, as well as create a plan for what to do when life brings challenges you didn't expect.

With thirty days of time-saving tips and systems, plus 101 time-saving tips tucked into the thirty chapters, you can begin having the time of your life. You will be more conscious of how you spend your time, who you spend it with, how you squander some of it, and how you wish to reorder it. In other words, you'll be in charge of your time instead of your time being in charge of you.

What Does It Mean to Simplify Your Time?

Simplifying your time involves managing yourself in regard to your available time to accomplish your goals at a reasonable pace. Once you start applying the principles in this book, you'll be able to simplify your time to stop running and start living.

With more time as your sought-after treasure, you can

- divide it;
- multiply it;
- supersize it;
- minimize it;
- evaluate it;
- delegate it;
- reassign it;

As we begin our journey to simplify your time, we are going on a hunt—for your "time" diamond. Time is the basis of all that you do and want to do. Let's find the time problems and time solutions that will simplify your life—starting today!

Decision Statement

I want to make my life better—and I believe the place to start is learning how to spend my time more effectively. I'm willing to go on a "diamond hunt" to find the solution to my time challenges for thirty days.

I want to simplify my life by simplifying my time. And I'm determined to make the necessary changes by taking this four week 30-day journey. After all, this *is* the time of my life!

_____   _____
Your Signature   Start Date

The highest reward for a person's toil is not what
they get for it, but what they become by it.

—John Ruskin

Time-Saving Habits to Simplify Your Daily Life

This week's time-saving habits will help you pinpoint ways you may be losing time each day—and how you can save more. Measure your current success against each of these chapters and start saving time by developing healthy daily habits.

WEEK 1
Time-Saving Habits to Simplify Your Daily Life

Day 2	Punch Up Your Punctuality
Day 3	Save Time with Two-Minute Pickups
Day 4	Get Off Your Computer and On with Your Life
Day 5	Power Through Your Paperwork
Day 6	Clean Up the Clutter
Day 7	Plan Tomorrow the Night Before
Day 8	Change a Habit, Change Your Life

Day 2

Punch Up
Your Punctuality

Bad habits are really nothing more than the wrong decision
made over and over. So always decide to be early.

—Diana DeLonzor

Ellen, a top-notch newspaper reporter, dashed into the restaurant brushing the
snow off her coat, unwrapping her scarf, and clearing her fogged glasses. She
looked like a Ferris wheel out of control as she caught herself from falling into
the front counter. She shifted her purse and notebook in front of her and
scanned the room.

When she spotted me, she hurried over and slid into the booth while her
litany of excuses tumbled out. "I'm so sorry I'm late, Marcia. Just what I
needed: to be late for an appointment with a professional organizer . . . to write
an article on getting organized. This is the story of my life. I really want to find
out how to change it. Maybe we'll start there. By the way, thanks for coming."
She sighed. "And how are you today?"

I have to confess I was more like Ellen in my past than she knew. I battled a lifelong habit of sliding into places just in time rather than on time or early. And I knew right where the problem began.

Five Sources of and Solutions to Chronic Lateness

Over the years, I discovered several sources of chronic lateness. I shared with Ellen that "on-time" people may view being late as a character flaw, but it is more complicated than that. The punctually challenged person may not know the source, yet identifying what is causing our lateness is the first step to finding the solution. Becoming aware can help us make the needed changes.

1. THE CAR RUNS OUT OF GAS AND YOUR WALLET IS EMPTY. Ellen ran into two problems on her way to the restaurant: she needed gas in her car and she didn't have a dime in her pocket to pay for coffee. So she borrowed ten dollars from a coworker and ran the two blocks in the snow.

Time-saving solution: Plan a dependable schedule for banking and gas. Fill your gas tank on the weekend so the car is ready on Monday morning. Do your banking on a regular day at the end of the week.

2. YOU FORGET TO SUBTRACT TIME TO GET READY. If it's 10:00 a.m. and you need to be at a luncheon at noon, how much time do you have to continue working? If your response is two hours, that may be the problem, because late people don't subtract the time needed to get ready and drive to their destination. In Ellen's case, twelve o'clock registered as the next event, and the arrival time became the departure time.

Time-saving solution: Use the "On your mark, get set, go!" principle. Just as a track coach shouts, "On your mark, get set, go!" so should you remind yourself to get ready. Subtract thirty minutes for closing your activities, gathering your things, and traveling. Plan only one and a half more hours of work and you'll meet your goal of being on time at noon.

The "On Your Mark, Get Set, Go!" Principle

....

- "On your mark"—This is the time to stop the activity you are doing, close your e-mail, and put things away.

- "Get set"—This is the transition time needed to think about what you'll need for the next event, collect your things, and get ready to leave.
- "Go!"—This is the time to walk out the door and drive off so you'll arrive early.

3. YOUR CLEANUP TENDENCY KICKS IN. While it is normal to clean up before you leave, this is not the time to go through your in-box, delete unnecessary e-mails, and label a file folder so you show up with a tidy set of papers in tow.

Time-saving solution: Write a "next actions" note. Jot a note before you leave, reminding yourself of your next steps. That will make it easy to resume your unfinished task when you return. Don't sabotage arriving at your destination by perfecting your desk or your appearance. Allow five extra minutes for touch-ups. Then leave.

4. YOU THINK THAT "TRANSITION TIME" TAKES NO TIME. Another common problem is ignoring the time it takes to actually get out the door and to your destination. Allow yourself the few minutes you need to find a coupon, get your sunglasses, fill your briefcase, close the blinds, lock the doors, and make sure the dog is OK.

Time-saving solution: Set aside time for routine "out-the-door" tasks. These "out-the-door" transitional tasks are often the culprit that turns being on time to being late. Estimate how long they take, and add those minutes to the overall time needed. Practice your accuracy.

5. YOU DON'T OWN UP TO YOUR EMOTIONS. When you are fuming over being late, check your emotions. What are they telling you about this event? For example, perhaps you feel anxious when you're around a certain person who asks too many questions, and you think you can avoid him or her if you arrive a few minutes late.

Time-saving solution: Acknowledge your emotions and work through them. If one person seems invasive with questions, plan a general answer such as, "Thanks for asking. Things are going well. How about you?" or "How are your kids?" Polite small talk will distract nosy people and fills in the time until the meeting starts.

How Do "On-Time" People Do It?

Did you know that "on-time" people think differently than late people? They do, and so can you. One high school band director, Warren Torns, had this advice for his six hundred players: "To be early is to be on time. To be on time is to be late. And to be late is unacceptable." By following this simple rule, his band was nationally recognized for excellence.

Tracy, a single working woman, says, "I go early to social events so I can catch up with my friends." She always makes people feel glad they came because she is there early greeting them with her smile and peaceful demeanor.

Harry, a busy manager, makes it to work early every day. "I'd rather arrive early than having the stress of being late," he says frankly. He sets the pace for his family by talking with each of his kids and getting out the door on time.

Ten Practical Tips for Being on Time

1. Always keep car keys, purse, and backpack on hooks and a shelf by the exit door.
2. Keep a clock in a prominent location so you can check it quickly when you have to leave your activities to be on time.
3. Clean out your purse or briefcase each evening so it's ready to go the next morning.
4. Know how much money is in your wallet so you won't run out of cash at an awkward time.
5. Check and fill your gas tank on a regular schedule, such as a quarter tank every Friday before the weekend prices go up.
6. Give up that "one last thing" before walking out the door to be on time.

7. Think about what you could do with an extra five minutes for every place where you arrived early. Consider it a bonus of an hour a week or more.

8. Put CDs you want to listen to in the car—an incentive to get your drive under way.   GOURMET !

9. Review your plans and to-dos for the rest of the day and make note of things that have changed.

10. Arrive early and reward yourself for the stress you saved by enjoying a cup of coffee or briefly calling a friend.

You can simplify your time by dropping the stress of arriving late. Start living by enjoying the five minutes you gain from being early. You actually do more harm to yourself with stress and guilt by working up to the last possible moment than by preparing to leave with time to spare. As a bonus, people will respect you for being dependable, which is an admirable character trait that shows you respect yourself and others.

Being on time is a habit worth acquiring and practicing. Not only will it improve your life, but it will influence others to respond by being reliable as well. And not only would that cut our waiting time in half each day, each week, and each year, but we could all experience more free time at the end of the day!

> ## Time-Saving Tip #6
>
> However early or late you arrive for your first event will set the pace for your day. Arrive early once, and repeat the pattern all day long.

It's Your Time

Punch Up Your Punctuality (Time Habit #1)

☐ Start a calendar to keep track of being "on time" for one particular event each day (e.g., arriving at work, leaving work, or eating dinner).

☐ Aspire to be on time twenty-one times in a row, and then reward yourself for a making a new time habit.

☐ Notice the benefits of being on time, and practice relaxing while doing so.

We are what we repeatedly do. Excellence, then,
is not an act, but a habit.

—Aristotle

Save Time with Two-Minute Pickups

One of the most valuable skills of time management is learning to use time fragments—the ten minutes waiting in line, the twenty minutes waiting for a meal, the thirty minutes riding somewhere, etc.

—Don Aslett

What do you do on days when you're especially rushed? If you're like most people, you double your speed, take shortcuts, and skim from one event to the next. But does it work?

Sometimes yes, but over the long term it creates more problems. Why? Because generally such actions leave a trail of unfinished tasks lingering behind you, including to-dos to follow up on, half-opened mail, and a dozen "quick" e-mails and voice messages to return, all of which nibble at your peace of mind.

Time-Saving Tip #7

Two-minute pickups are tasks that are too short to write on a to-do list but that slow the pace of your life when they are ignored too long.

Is there a solution? Yes, if you regularly practice the time-saving habit of using two-minute pickups to clean up and bring closure to a task. Perfect them, and you will simplify your time at home, at work, and on the run.

A Two-Minute Pickup Becomes a Two-Minute Solution

Ron pushed through the crowd at the end of one of my sessions on organizing time. "Well, Marcia," he began, "you've done it. You've motivated me to do something my mother and my ex-wife have spent twenty years in vain trying to get me to do."

"What could that possibly be?"

"Make my bed every day. When you said, 'Make your bed and make your day,' I wondered if you were for real. But when you said it only takes ninety seconds to pull up the covers on one side, then the other, and plop the pillows on, I thought, *I could do that!* And you said it makes 50 to 70 percent of the room look neat and clean for sixteen hours of the day. That makes sense. I have to make the bed at night anyway before I get back in it."

I chuckled. Such a little thing was a big deal for Ron. His two-minute pickup became a two-minute solution for a relational problem he didn't even know he had.

Ron found that once he mastered one two-minute pickup, he looked for more two-minute solutions. He began at home and reported to me a couple of weeks later that the place was looking pretty "shipshape."

When I saw him next, he had a fresh haircut and looked sharp. He had found the time to take care of himself and started to be more positive. The routine of making his bed every day started the momentum to get the rest of his life in order—in two-minute segments.

Time-Saving Tip #8

A two-minute solution for a recurring task saves ten minutes every time thereafter. You could save five hours a month or sixty hours in one year for a short two-minute investment.

---

simplify your time

Save Time at Home

Here are some two-minute solutions to help you save time at home:

- Load the dishwasher.
- Water a plant.
- Renew a prescription.
- Pay a bill.
- Program a cell phone number.
- RSVP.
- Fold the laundry.

Do a few of these each day, and you just may save enough time to sit down for a cup of coffee and watch the sun set!

Save Time at Work

My client Melinda had control of her time at home, but she was always rushed at work. "I consistently misplace my agenda for our staff meetings—and I lead them!" Melinda agonized. "I waste time looking for last week's agenda so I can use it to write a new one and then make copies for everyone. Why can't they hire an assistant to do that for me? I should be doing more important things."

Melinda was under the false assumption that because of her "big" title, small tasks shouldn't be her responsibility. In a way that was true, but writing the agenda and leading the meeting were part of her leadership role.

I wanted to be kind but firm in my response. "Time to take another look at this situation, OK? Be realistic. It's unprofessional and unfair to expect an assistant to do for you what you can and should do for yourself. No one can read your mind. By taking charge, you also reap the benefits. Things will get done your way. What have you tried so far?"

Melinda admitted, "I tried a notebook, but then I misplaced it. I failed at filing because I hate to file. But I'd better do something—fast. My boss is

"MEETING BINDER" — MASTER COPIES — BLANK COPIES — PAST FILED COPIES

> **Time-Saving Tip #9**
>
> If it only takes two minutes to complete a simple task, continue this practice twenty-one times and you will develop a habit you can depend on.

expecting a report on the steps I've taken to finish our team project."

In our discussion, Melinda narrowed the solution to two choices: either she could get a new file to store her previous agendas (a colored one clearly labeled to help her spot it quickly), or she could keep a paper punch on her credenza. When needed, all she had to do was spin around and punch the pages before snapping them into her three-ring binder. With either solution, she could make a second copy of the previous week's agenda to place in a two-pocket folder for safekeeping.

"I like the idea of walking into the meeting with a binder and being able to refer to past meetings," she decided. "I can pick up a three-hole punch in the supply room. Why didn't I think of that?"

At work, there are many two-minute pickups that will save you time and energy. Consider the following:

- Reply to and close any open e-mail.
- File the paperwork on your desk.
- Replace an old file folder.
- Label a binder.
- Pick up a fax and file it.
- Prioritize your in-box.
- Check off your completed to-do list items.

Put a few of these to work, and you'll feel more energetic and in control at the end of the day.

Moving Ahead

You might be wondering what became of Melinda. I have good news. She started labeling and filing the mess of papers on her desk, one set each day. In less than a month, her desktop was clear, and she had regained confidence and control.

The next time we met, I asked her how she was doing. She laughed with relief. "When I realized what a time-saver my meeting binder was, I decided to apply the same strategy to other areas. Now my projects, my expense reports, basically everything on my desk is in order and easy to find."

As two-minute pickups become part of your daily routine, you, too, will experience wonderful benefits at home and at work. You'll be more relaxed, orderly, and efficient.

Practice sensing how long two minutes are by heating a cup of tea in your microwave for two minutes and seeing what you can do in that time. Soon it will be part of your time-saving routine. And then you can sit and enjoy your tea.

> **Time-Saving Tip #10**
>
> How much time will I save with a new habit?
> Time Spent: 2 minutes x 21 days = 42 minutes setting up a solution
> Time Saved: 10 minutes x 21 days = 3.5 hours of stress-free rewards

Like Interest on a Loan, Time Compounds Every Day

When you think about it, if you spend two minutes bringing one item to closure, you will save at least ten minutes to use in some other way. Compounded over longer periods of time, this really adds up.

You can work your way out of stressful situations by investing two minutes several times a day on a consistent basis. Reap the reward at the end of each month with more solutions to problems that once drained your energy. Make two-minute pickups a part of your lifestyle, and by the end of the year you'll have saved hundreds of hours that you can use to relax, work on your hobby, play golf, or take a class.

So what are you waiting for? Start now. Simplify your time by picking up the pace in every area of your life. Ask yourself all day long, "What can I do with two minutes?" And then do it!

It's Your Time
Save Time with Two-Minute Pickups (Time Habit #2)

☐ Learn *not* to put things down but to put them away all day to simplify your life.

☐ Practice the two-minute pickup before you leave a room or work area.

☐ Learn to decide it, do it, schedule it, sign it, end it, or send it in two minutes all day long.

Nothing is beneath you if it is in the direction of your life.

—Ralph Waldo Emerson

Day 4

Get Off Your Computer and On with Your Life

Think about it: E-mail is really nothing but a bunch of interruptions and distractions that appear in your in box without an invitation. Even checking your e-mail for a minute is a surefire way to . . . distract your mind with a zillion other issues. Once that happens, prolonged concentration on anything, critical or not, is nearly impossible.

—Julie Morgenstern

Kay sighed and turned out the light at her desk—not at the office but at home. Everyone else in the family had gone to bed long ago. Lately she had been the last one shutting down her computer, locking the doors, and turning out the lights.

Kay shared this dilemma with me when we met at one of my seminars. She leaned forward, eager to vent her frustration. "I can't keep up with my e-mail no matter how determined I am not to let it control my time," she said. "I even turn on my computer first thing in the morning to get a head start. I've got to get back to my life! What can I do?"

Millions of men and women have the same problem. What began as a convenience has become a compulsion. Following are some ideas I offered Kay. I hope they will work for you too.

You Conquered Junk Mail, Now Conquer E-mail

It wasn't long ago that junk mail made up most of our clutter. The average household, for example, receives fifteen pieces of mail each day. You can shred the junk mail, file the important bills and papers, and distribute the rest until all are in their rightful places, or you can let them clutter up your counter or desk. E-mail is much the same way. You need to decide how to get rid of the junk e-mail, handle the important items, and dispense with the medium priorities so they don't clutter up your in-box.

So why is e-mail so difficult? That's a good question. It's difficult because we are relational and emotional beings. And just as curiosity killed the proverbial cat, we are drawn to check our e-mail "one more time." We could just get up and walk away, but we don't. Messages arrive quickly, and we want to find out what they're about, who sent them, and what we need to respond to. We remain expectant all day long—sometimes for as much as sixteen hours. Then we wonder why we didn't accomplish any of our priorities.

> **Time-Saving Tip #11**
>
> Schedule e-mail sessions at regular times, such as 10:00 a.m., 2:00 p.m., and 5:00 p.m. Plan to spend twenty minutes each time or one hour a day. If that's not enough, decide how much is and stick to it.

Is Your Computer Controlling Your Life?

Only you can answer that question. Whether you turn on your computer for work, for personal correspondence, or as a first response to walking into your office or computer room, there is a better way to live.

If you get up from your computer session with a brain fog or irritated that your life is slower than the speed of your computer, it's time to slow down.

Your E-mail In-Box

How many e-mails do you receive each day? According to a survey of 2,447 adults conducted by the Pew Internet and American Life Project, there are two kinds of e-mailers: the "average user" and the "power user." Following are the results of this survey:

	Incoming E-mails	Sent	Time
Average User	20	5	30 minutes
Power User	50+	20+	90 minutes
Your Statistics			

Five Ways to Get Off E-mail

Kay considered herself an average user, but she still found it difficult to get off her computer. Here are five ways that could be helpful to Kay and perhaps to you, if your e-mail habits are escalating out of control.

1. NEVER CHECK E-MAIL IN THE MORNING. According to Julie Morgenstern, author of a book by that same title, you will be more productive if you spend the first hour of the day on concentrated work items apart from e-mail. Then when time's up, turn on the e-mail and begin.

2. IMPROVE YOUR SORTING METHOD. Systematically deal with e-mail each day. Don't skip around.

- Send junk e-mail to the "blocked senders" list.
- Respond to key people and projects.
- Start at the top and respond to messages that require two minutes or less.
- Place remainders in folders by person or project.
- Follow up on longer responses the next time you open your e-mail.

3. CREATE FOLDERS WITH TIME LIMITS. Deal with your e-mail folders on a regular basis.

- Delete File—Empty on Fridays at the end of the day.
- Temporary File—Empty on Friday after using this file as a temporary holding place for the week.
- Read File—Read midafternoon for a workday break.
- Important File—Hold these for a longer term and review at the end of the month.

Time-Saving Tip #12

Send regular distribution news e-mails the same time and same day each week. People will appreciate your regularity.

4. TITLE YOUR E-MAILS ACCURATELY. Don't waste people's time by hitting Reply before you relabel the subject line. Instead, pride yourself on accuracy and write a short title of what is to follow: "Project Due Tues. Noon" or "Hi, Mom, What's for Dinner?"

5. TIME IT, TRACK IT, FINE-TUNE IT. One day, jot down each time you check your e-mail. You may find that you impulsively hit Send/Receive more often than necessary. Next, track it for three days and fine-tune your times until e-mail is just a part of your day, not your whole day.

Tips from Power Users

Thousands of people have mastered the use of their computers, and you can too. Pay attention to the men and women you know who accomplish the most in life. What kind of e-mails do they send? Check their efficiency, clarity, and brevity. Follow their example. Why not learn and imitate the best of what comes across your screen?

Here are some of the key strategies and habits of "power users":

- Their answers are brief.
- They get right to the point.
- They are known for quick responses.

- They provide pertinent information.
- They do not waste time sending forwards.
- They keep a file of stock answers for FAQs (frequently asked questions).

What Will I Do When I Get Off My Computer?

It sounds like a funny question, but unless you plan what you'll do when you finally shut down your computer, you'll linger and check for more e-mail, research your project longer, or continue to browse and waste more time.

Instead, set a timer to get yourself up, go for a walk, pull away for a brief rest, and eat regularly scheduled meals. Set boundaries with coworkers and with yourself so you will leave work on time. Go to the gym a few times a week to avoid carpal tunnel syndrome and back and neck pain. These actions will also keep you from wearing the letters off your keyboard!

Only you can decide when too much is too much. If you are serious about curbing your hours at the computer, you'll need a plan to keep yourself motivated. Otherwise, you'll be drawn back like a magnet to steel. Precious time wasted in front of a computer may turn out to be the primary hindrance to getting on with your life.

> **Time-Saving Tip #13**
>
> Be proactive in averting junk e-mail by not just deleting it but instead sending it to a "blocked senders" list that will delete and block future e-mails from this source.

Simplify Your Time and Get On with Your Life

Isn't it interesting that when computers first came on the scene, most of us were afraid of pushing a key or button that could result in a crash? Now the pendulum has swung the other way. We're afraid (or at least resistant) of pushing the Off button so we can get on with the rest of our lives.

If the computer has become your life—stop. Pull away from your monitor, close the door, and do something you enjoy away from the screen and keyboard.

It's Your Time

Get Off Your Computer and On with Your Life (Time Habit #3)

☐ What is your personal red flag that you have been on the computer too long (e.g., resenting others who work fewer hours, feeling mentally stressed when I get off, etc.)?

☐ Track your computer hours for today (or one week) to discover your actual time.

☐ What would you like to be doing instead of being on the computer?

It is not how many e-mails you get. It is how many you let "hang around"! Your "In Box" is not a filing cabinet, a to-do list, a calendar, an address book, or a bookmark list. Although you have limited control over the number of e-mails you get, you have total control over the number you leave in your "In Box." . . . Keep your In Box empty!"

—Barbara Hemphill

Power Through
Your Paperwork

Up to 70 percent of a magazine is advertisements and they
are updated every month, so you don't need to keep them.
. . . If there happens to be an article you want to read or
save, tear it out and read or file it, and throw the rest away.

—Don Aslett

"Your daughter is on the phone," Danielle's secretary announced over the
intercom. Danielle ended her conversation with her boss and took the call.

"Mom," her nine-year-old daughter Gabrielle started, sniffling at the other
end, "my class is going to the planetarium today, but the teacher won't let me
go without my permission slip. Did you forget to sign it?"

Danielle sighed. Yes, she meant to sign and return it right away, but she must
have gotten distracted. It was sitting in the pile of papers on the kitchen counter—
or was it by the computer? "Let me talk with your teacher," said Danielle.

Gabrielle turned the phone over to Mrs. Dartmouth, but before Danielle
could begin, the teacher broke in. "Mrs. Jones, this is the third time you've

Time-Saving Tip #14

Allow twenty minutes
to process (read, file
and do) the daily
mail. Or plan two
hours on the weekend
to catch up.

missed a permission slip deadline. I'm sorry, but it's too late now. The bus is filled. Please pick up Gabrielle at the office."

Danielle felt reprimanded as she left work. She realized it was her fault, one more in a long string of mishaps. Her boss was irritated because two weeks ago she took off to get her son's passport notarized for his trip to Europe—the day it was due.

Those two paperwork problems took two mornings to unravel, but there was another one that kept her awake at night. Danielle explained it to me on the phone. "I turned in my taxes really late this year," she stated. "But I've got to have that refund check this week or borrow money, which I can't afford. Why does everything depend on paperwork?"

Paper, Paper, Everywhere

If it's true that people spend twenty minutes a day looking for things, it's likely that fifteen minutes of that time is spent searching for a missing paper. Danielle lost two mornings of work taking care of her kids' paperwork, several weeks of sleepless nights waiting for her refund check, and frequent moments of disrespect from her boss, a teacher, and her children. It was getting costly.

Here's what Danielle needed to know to turn things around and put things in place.

Clean Up the Mail Pile Every Day

The average household receives fifteen pieces of mail a day. Five of those are junk mail and can be tossed immediately. Likely, five more are bills or important papers you can file appropriately. And the other five, which I call the "dangling five," start a paper pile on the kitchen counter.

In a year of five extra papers a day on the counter, fifteen hundred to eighteen hundred pieces of paper, or fifteen to eighteen inches of paperwork, pile up and send you scrambling to find the one paper you need when you need it. That's no longer necessary if you establish a workable plan to handle your mail.

Set Up a Personal Organizing Center

Danielle and I set up a Personal Organizing Center (POC) in the kitchen right near her monthly calendar and telephone. The two feet of counter space became the sole spot to open mail and handle the day's papers.

All the daily papers landed there. In a drawer she kept a small black office tray divider with a working pen and pencil, two sizes of paper clips, stamps, Post-it notes, and highlighters for reading newsletters quickly. "This is neat," Danielle exclaimed. "Everything I need to do my paperwork is available. But what do I do with the paper?"

Five File Folders Save the Day

I explained to Danielle how five file folders could help her keep track of papers.

FOLDER #1—**Calendar.** This holds any paper that relates to an event on your calendar. No more refrigerator clutter.

FOLDER #2—**To Do.** If an item takes five minutes or less, then do it right now. If longer, write it on a master to-do list you keep visible. Write the tasks on the three days you can most control—today, tomorrow, and the day after. Beyond that, you never know when you'll have time to do them.

FOLDER #3—**To Decide.** This file contained everything Danielle was thinking about doing but wasn't yet ready to do. It cleared a lot of paperwork off the countertop.

FOLDER #4—**Information.** This file held carpool lists, the neighborhood calling tree, and the soccer schedule to retrieve at a moment's notice.

FOLDER #5—**My Interests.** Here Danielle dropped in a free fitness center coupon, a decorator's advertisement, and a phone number for a landscaper. When she had time, she would turn to this file and decide which things she was ready to attend to.

> ### Time-Saving Tip #15
>
> Spend five minutes labeling the five folders to save you five minutes every time you need to locate a paper.

A Place for Everything and Every Paper in Its Place

We sorted the rest of the papers and decided where to store them and how long to keep them.

Paper	Where to Keep It?	How Long?
Morning newspaper	Coffee table	Until noon
School newsletter	File #4 —Information	Until the next one comes out
Children's finished papers—save the best, toss the rest	A three-ring binder "Memory Book"	End of school year or permanently in binder
Bills to pay	Small desk drawer	Pay online or by hand the fifth of the month.
Utility bills	File folder in desk	Until balanced since last bill
Mortgage payments	File folder in desk	Seven years for tax records
Magazines	A magazine holder or coffee table	New one in, old one out, even if you have to read it on the spot.
Newsletters	Read it with the day's mail or file by organization.	New one in, old one out. There is no "later" to read.
Bulletins	File #1—Calendar	New one in, old one out.
A good article	File #5—Personal	Date it with the day/month/year and source.
Coupons	Coupon holder	Keep only items you use.
A new recipe	Recipe file	Date, file, and save under "To Try" for three months.

simplify your time

Danielle was getting more and more excited as she put each paper in a file folder, the magazine holder, or the recycle bin. "There is a place for everything, isn't there?"

"Yes, and if there isn't, you can create a system holder for it. When everything gets filed each day," I reminded her, "either once a day when the mail comes in or before leaving work, your retrieval time savings multiplies without piles to wade through."

Customize Your Files or Binders

Danielle and her children created a two-pocket folder—green for Gabrielle and blue for Keith—with the right pocket designated for the work that came home from school and the left pocket for completed homework and papers to return to school.

Each night after dinner, the kids went through their folders while Danielle finished kitchen cleanup. She stopped filling in forms they could handle without help, such as name, address, and phone number, and only filled out the ones that required her signature or had information specifically for a parent.

Danielle charged them one dollar for any extra trips she had to make to school or for papers signed the day they were due. Gabrielle and Keith quickly became responsible.

On-Time Paperwork Saves You Time and Money

Danielle felt a burden lift as she found another permission slip due the next day, a sizable missing check to cash, and her best friend's birthday card. "This is exciting!" she declared. "I'm going to be on time with my paperwork, and I will pay bills online each month. I never thought of late paperwork as lost time or money.

Time-Saving Tip #16

Act on any paper-related item that takes five minutes or less. Place the others on a master list and do them on the three days you can most control—today, tomorrow, and the next day.

Time-Saving Tip #17

Every paper problem has a solution. Ask, "What is the next action I need to take with this paper?" Then trim the FAT: File, Act, or Toss.

"Keeping up on my paperwork each day is the best time-saver of all. I can read my magazines and not worry about what I might have missed doing. I can do this!"

It's Your Time
Power Through Your Paperwork (Time Habit #4)

To set up a Personal Organizing Center, do the following:
- ☐ Create five file folders.
- ☐ Keep paperwork supplies handy.
- ☐ Designate a bin for shredding and recycling.
- ☐ Go through your paperwork until your desk or counter is clean.

Remember that today's mail is tomorrow's pile. Take today's mail to your paper-management center and begin now to develop your own paper-management system.

—Barbara Hemphill

Day 6

Clean Up the Clutter

Don't let the fear of the time it will take to accomplish
something stand in the way of your doing it. The time
will pass anyway; we might just as well put that
passing time to the best possible use.

—Earl Nightingale

"Who wants to go out for ice cream?" my husband asked on a Sunday summer evening. Our three children immediately responded, "Meeeeeeeeeee!!!"

I chuckled at their enthusiasm despite the long day we'd had, including the hassle of breakfast, church, lunch, and dinner with young children. As a matter of fact, I relaxed a little myself all day and left the dishes in the kitchen sink. But as I thought about time out for ice cream, I spied the sink full of dishes I had left from the day.

"David, why don't you take the kids, and I'll clean up and enjoy a little time for myself?" My husband nodded, knowing it would give me a break. I thought I'd spend about half an hour on the dishes and then read a magazine or relax a bit before the busy week ahead.

As I washed dishes, I thought about how this simple task used to take all evening. With no plan and lots of interruptions, it became a never-ending process. At least now I had shortened it to ten minutes after every meal. *So three meals today should only take thirty minutes,* I told myself. I started the dishwasher, cleaned the pans, wiped down the counters, and swept the floor. When I sat down and glanced at the clock, I was surprised. It had taken me an hour and a half!

My rest was short-lived as the family came piling in a few minutes later. I missed my entire break time—over what? A day's worth of dishes. How disappointing to miss ice cream *and* peace and quiet.

At that moment I suddenly saw what I had not seen before, and a time principle was forever etched in my mind. *Maintenance is always more effective and efficient than a big cleanup.* What should have taken thirty minutes took three times as long! That's a real time waster.

You, too, can save time by putting away household clutter of dishes, laundry, and paperwork as you go. Here are three systems to streamline cleaning up the clutter at home.

Quick Cleanups Save Time

It takes only one step to put an item away immediately after using it. But it takes two steps to use an item and set it down before putting it back later. Here are some examples of short cleanups:

- Hang up your coat when you take it off instead of dropping it on the couch.
- Put your bags, mail, and briefcase away when you walk through the door instead of dropping them on a counter.
- Put your paperwork away when you're finished instead of leaving it out.

A Quick Pickup Each Morning and Evening Saves Time

I'm always looking for faster ways to save time and keep a nice-looking home. The best way I've found is to notice which efforts keep my personal pace in order with the least amount of effort.

System #1: Morning Cleanup Routine
1. Make the beds: 2 minutes each
2. Pick up the bathrooms: 5 minutes
3. Clean up the kitchen: 15 minutes

When I asked an audience of preschool mothers what happens after the morning routine of making beds, picking up the bathrooms, and cleaning up the kitchen, one mom with a newborn and two toddlers raised her hand and answered, "Lunch?"

After the audience had a good chuckle, I reassured her the three hours of household chores between nine and twelve would shorten to thirty minutes or less once the children were older and able to do more things for themselves. Good routines improve as you practice getting better results, all with an eye to creating your own time-saving shortcuts.

System #2: Evening Cleanup Routine
1. Complete the mail: 15 minutes
2. Put away laundry: 10 minutes
3. Pick up clutter: 10 minutes

When you pick up clutter and put away personal and household items each day, you follow the same principle I learned when I missed my ice cream outing: maintenance takes two-thirds less time than a big cleanup.

A Time-Saving Weekly Schedule

Save yourself additional time by planning the tasks you have to do each week to keep your life running smoothly. These might include banking, errands, filing, emptying wastebaskets, and completing projects. Sometimes it feels like more than we can handle. But when you put the tasks on paper, they become less daunting.

System #3: The Weekly Cleaning Routine
Weekly Cleaning Strategic Tasks
1. Empty trash cans.
2. Change bed linens.
3. Vacuum traffic areas.
4. Mop or sweep the kitchen and bathroom floors.
5. Eliminate an annoying pile.
6. Complete a project from your project list.
7. Include banking, fueling your car, and shopping in your weekly plan.

Don't Just Think About It—Take Action!

Time-Saving Tip #19

Pick up items each morning and evening and save two-thirds the time it takes to do a major cleanup on the weekend.

Making a list is a great idea, but your chance of finishing the tasks on that list will be reduced by 50 percent unless you link it to your calendar or other time management system. For the most productive use of your time, assign a task to a particular day of the week and stick to it.

Save time and eliminate worry and stress by doing the same tasks on the same day each week. Your schedule will then "decide" for you the "when" and "what." Just do it and be done.

simplify your time

Visible and Invisible Clutter

There are two kinds of clutter: visible and invisible. The visible clutter sits out on your countertops, desk, and tables, while the invisible clutter is hidden behind closed cabinets, closets, and drawers. Both kinds can slow you down and sap your mental and emotional energy.

For instance, if you have clutter on your countertops, and you spend five minutes a day looking for an item, that's 30.4 hours a year spent looking for something in a drawer or paper pile. Think about it. You could have an extra three days each year to use in a more enjoyable way if you just put things away. What great motivation to clean up the clutter!

Find a "Giveaway" Spot and Fill It

What if you want to get rid of something in order to simplify your life? It would waste time to drive to Salvation Army only to deliver one extra curling iron. So what can you do?

Save time by designating a "giveaway" spot in your garage or closet with neatly marked boxes, such as the following:

- giveaway clothes
- giveaway stuff (items other than clothing)
- giveaway media (books, CDs, and DVDs)

You can choose whether to give these items away to a charity or needy family, or you could sell them in a garage sale. One time I sold several boxes of items at a friend's garage sale over the course of two weekends. With the earned income we bought a new light fixture for our foyer. But more important, I saved a total of 12.5 hours for the year by not spending five minutes per item to clean, sort, or store the things we sold or gave away. That's time saved and freedom gained.

Time-Saving Tip #20

One of the fastest ways to save time is to do the same thing at the same time every week. Soon it will be a habit—the kind that works in your favor.

Schedule quarterly charity pickups on your calendar to keep down the clutter you have to put away. Clean out closets in the fall and spring to contribute unused clothing.

my class participants, Jan Hickerson, a R   s getting ready to move. She shared how she   ll the unopened tools and products her husband   ed and, with his permission, returned them to   Depot. She proudly displayed the credit slip for   nd enjoyed the cleared space.

friend of mine interviewed a cleaning lady who   ed to work for her unless she put away some of the   y collectibles she had on display. Chris learned some-   ng from the experience. "I never realized how much   utter these items added to our living space. Marcia,   ou'd be proud of me. My home is now uncluttered and   easier to keep in order—and I have saved a great deal of cleaning time each week."

It's Your Time
Clean Up the Clutter (Time Habit #5)

☐ Commit to cleaning one stressful area regularly (e.g., kitchen papers or laundry).

☐ Find "homes" for homeless items that pile up.

☐ Put away clutter every day until your counters and floors are clean and clutter free.

Creating open space is a two-step process. First, clear clutter from all flat surfaces one at a time. That includes the desktop, counter, table, shelf, windowsill, floor, and any other surfaces. After you have cleared all the flat surfaces, then you begin to delve into the inner spaces: drawers, cupboards, closets.

—Porter Knight

Day 7

Plan Tomorrow
the Night Before

Tomorrow we will become what we choose today.

—John Maxwell

I was chatting with a women's director when one of her ladies joined us. "Excuse me, Stephanie, I just wanted to let you know that I won't be able to come to lunch today. It's been such a busy week—extra time at school, my son got sick, and I'm behind at home—that I haven't had time to spend time with my mother, and her birthday was last weekend. So I need to be with her. Let me know when you have it next time. I'll be sure to come."

As the woman walked away, Stephanie looked stunned. "Can you believe that? The hostess has a gorgeous home and planned a luxurious luncheon at her own expense so we could meet together. We only had six women coming, and this lady tells me she can't come the hour before? Why couldn't she at least have called yesterday? That's just inconsiderate. Grr!"

When you simplify your time, one of the most considerate steps you can take is to plan tomorrow the night before. This saves yourself and other people time. And it keeps you in everyone's good graces.

Set Up Tomorrow for Success

Anyone can develop the habit of preparing for tomorrow the night before. You're set up for a good day when you have items placed in a regular "launching spot" and appointments confirmed as soon as possible.

My husband saves time by neatly zipping up his computer case with his papers inside at the foot of the stairs at night. He has a mental checklist of items laid out on his dresser to take: his watch, his work badge, and his favorite pen. He has never had a bad day because of a forgotten necessity.

I began the practice of calling clients the day before our meeting to find out the top three to five issues they wanted to cover, to answer questions and confirm the time, and to find out whether I should dress for organizing their garage or their paperwork. It relieved their fears and gave us a fast start when we got together.

Lucy, a busy executive, liked to have our daughter babysit overnight while she was on business but often missed getting Lisa because of waiting until the week of her travels to call. When Lucy learned to call immediately when a trip came up, she got her dependable sitter almost 100 percent of the time.

> **Time-Saving Tip #22**
>
> With so much to do every day, you can actually spend time getting more things done while spending less time doing them— if you plan tomorrow the night before.

Does Planning Take Time or Save Time?

Those who plan tomorrow the night before have learned it takes just a few minutes once they consistently practice the habit. Now they are no longer surprised that someone doesn't show up for lunch because they had it on the wrong week or they missed jury duty because they forgot.

At work, there are numerous ways to plan tomorrow the night before. Consider the following:

- Confirm tomorrow's appointments.
- E-mail your group, reminding participants of the meeting time, location, and agenda.

- Print all directions for sales calls, and confirm with the client the time and topics.
- Go through your in-box and list important items and time frames in which you'll handle them.
- Check with support staff on the status of project steps.
- Confirm due dates with team members.

At home, there are numerous ways to plan tomorrow the night before. Consider the following:

- Prepare your grocery list.
- Find your receipt to return an item.
- Pull together the dry cleaning to drop off.
- Schedule an online package pickup with your mail carrier.
- Get your old watch battery ready so you purchase the correct size.
- Call to confirm your babysitter.

The Rewards of Planning Ahead

The bonus for planning ahead is a successful day, meeting people on time instead of showing up to a locked door of someone who forgot an appointment with you. Errands get done when you gather materials the night before, so your clocks get fixed, lightbulbs get replaced, and you can stay home for the rest of the evening.

Driving Down the Highway of Life Management Skills

I learned to apply this time-saving principle to driving to new places. As helpful as an accurate set of directions is, I always focused on the next turn. But when I got off the freeway, I didn't know which way to turn without scrambling for my map while driving.

No more. I realized I could train myself to think of not just the next turn but the next two or even three turns. That's what you can do as you plan tomorrow: teach yourself to rehearse the next three things you are going to do during the day so you keep driving smoothly from one task to the next.

Planning sequentially the night before allows you to accomplish BOTH major tasks and minor necessities so all is complete by the end of the day. Remember, the most important time you spend in a day is the time you spend planning tomorrow.

Time-Saving Tip #23

Five minutes of planning the night before + five minutes of calling to confirm appointments = a successful tomorrow.

It's Your Time
Plan Tomorrow the Night Before (Time Habit #6)

☐ Call or e-mail to confirm your events for tomorrow.
☐ Keep a notepad at the same spot and write out tomorrow's tasks the night before.
☐ At night, review how well your day's list worked and improve the one for tomorrow.

Time-Saving Tip #24

Plan tomorrow on paper—with tasks and a time frame assigned for each of your top three priorities.

It takes time, effort, and the ability to overcome setbacks. You have to approach each day with reasonable expectations and not get your feelings hurt when everything doesn't turn out perfectly.

—John Maxwell

hange a Habit,
hange Your Life

Motivation is what gets you started.
Habit is what keeps you going.

—Jim Rohn

Jane paused thoughtfully over her coffee as we discussed time-saving habits. "I'd like to make all of these mine," she said, "but I don't know where to start." She listed the areas that were bogging her down—such as excess time on the computer, paper clutter, e-mail, and life in general. "When does catch-up time show up?" she asked. "I'd like to take a week off and get organized."

"I understand," I replied. "But you can't do it all at once. You can do it, however, by focusing on acquiring one habit during each of the four seasons." I showed her the chart below:

Jan.–March	April–June	July–Sept.	Oct.–Dec.
Being on Time	Limiting Computer Time	Completing Projects	Cutting Paper Clutter

"Oh, that's good," she replied. "I dream of walking out the door of an organized home in the morning, being on time, arriving at work to a clear desk, and having everything prepared for the day. And to think I could come home knowing what's for dinner? That would be the frosting on the cake. Is it possible?"

Yes, it's possible. But you have to know how to change your habits. A flurry of motivated efforts won't keep your paper piles clear once and for all any more than three nights of sit-ups would permanently flatten your stomach. Habits bend to follow the path of least resistance. Unless we shake them up and make some thoughtful choices, we'll maintain the good and bad habits we have today, making it more difficult to change in the future.

The results of good habits show up right away. Those of bad habits take longer to appear—but their consequences are greater.

> ### Time-Saving Tip #25
>
> It takes twenty-one repetitions to create a new habit. Save time by changing a bad habit into a new one starting today.

How Much Time Can a Good Habit Save?

If you can tighten up just one habit to save five or ten minutes a day, the effect over the long term would be outstanding. For example:

Daily	Weekly	Monthly	Yearly
5 minutes	35 minutes	2 hours, 20 minutes	30 hours
10 minutes	I hour, 10 minutes	4 hours, 40 minutes	60 hours
15 minutes	I hour, 45 minutes	7 hours	84 hours
20 minutes	2 hours, 20 minutes	9 hours, 20 minutes	112 hours

We'd all like to have an extra 112 hours sitting in a lump sum at the end of the year. Instead, it shows up as a cushion of time in your daily life. The time is there. We just have to figure out how to keep it from slipping away.

Create Good Habits, Drop the Old

According to Webster's dictionary, a *habit* is "a pattern of action that is acquired and has become so automatic that it is difficult to break." Many of us know it takes twenty-one days of consistent practice to form a new habit. That can take anywhere from three weeks to three months. Beyond that time frame, it will not stick!

A habit, good or bad, can save us time each day. Keeping your car keys in one spot, leaving at the same time for work, and going to bed at the same time each night are successful time habits that will keep you healthy and in good spirits. Putting money away in savings each month will ensure a lovely retirement. Time spent on good habits multiplies the same way.

If you are losing twenty minutes a day in some area of your life because of a poor habit, it's time to turn things around and replace it with a good habit.

> **Time-Saving Tip #26**
>
> A change in habit is an investment in a better future. Save ten minutes of morning indecision by creating a time plan for the next day.

How Can You Change a Habit?

You will change when your desire to change is greater than your desire to remain the same. It comes down to despising the pain more than the effort to make the change. Having a clear picture of what you want will catapult you forward toward tremendous success.

Write your desired changes as personal affirmations. Say them often enough, and soon they will become habits. Here are some examples of our seven time-saving habits:

1. "I arrive calmly and on time for my appointments."
2. "I save time by using two-minute pickups."
3. "I get off my computer at normal closing time each day."
4. "I power through my paperwork with confidence and clarity."
5. "I clean up clutter because I love the look of clean surfaces."

6. "I confirm appointments and line up items each night."
7. "I successfully change one habit at a time and enjoy the freedom it brings."

The Anatomy of a Realistic Twenty-one Times to Change a Habit

Anything that is measurable is changeable. Start by creating a chart with a spot for each of the twenty-one days. There are four levels to the process of creating a new habit by repeating it twenty-one times:

1–4 TIMES OF DOING A TASK—"I could do it if I just tried harder." Then old habits kick in with stress and time pressures. Keep going anyway.

5–10 TIMES—"I recognize the obstacles to doing it successfully." Then old habits kick in again and you feel like a failure. Just keep going.

11–15 TIMES—"I need to revisit my desired goal and focus on success." Old habits try to thwart you, but now you are determined. Keep going.

16–21 TIMES—"The goal is in sight, I know why I want it, and it is worth pushing through to success." You did it! Celebrate and enjoy your new habit.

HABIT CHANGE: COMPUTER TIME DOWN TO THIRTY-SIX HOURS A WEEK

Week	Mon.	Tues.	Wed.	Thurs.	Fri.	Sat.	Sun.	TOTAL
#1	9 hrs.	8 hrs.	4 hrs.	10 hrs.	9 hrs.	4 hrs.	3 hrs.	47 hrs.
#2	7 hrs.	8 hrs.	5 hrs.	9 hrs.	7 hrs.	2 hrs.	2 hrs.	40 hrs.
#3	8 hrs.	7 hrs.	4 hrs.	8 hrs.	7 hrs.	1 hr.	I hr.	36 hrs.

Then do it another twenty-one times to ensure permanent success. The best way to maintain a new habit is to strive for a "no-exceptions policy." Keep at it every day.

Habit Change: On-Time to Places 21 Times

Number the places from 1-21 you are on time until you reach your goal of 21. You will feel good and people will respect you more.

Mon.	Tues.	Wed.	Thurs.	Fri.	Sat.	Sun.	TOTAL
1 Dentist	2 PTA	3 Work	4 Work	0	5 Party	6 Church	1–6
7 Work	8 Staff	9 Lunch	10 Meeting	11 Staff	12 Soccer	13 Church	7–13
14 Work	15 Work	16 Work	17–18 Work Banquet	19 Work	20 Soccer	21 Church	21 Times!

What Makes a New Habit?

To make a new habit—one that is practiced routinely and automatically and is difficult to break—you need to work through a sequence:

Step #1: Identify which habit you are going to change.

Step #2. Recognize what the bad habit is costing you.

Step #3. Picture yourself accomplishing the new habit.

Step #4. Set a time to begin.

Step #5. Find a measurable accountability system or person.

Step #6. Recognize your weak point and find a way through it.

Step #7. Practice the new habit twenty-one times in succession.

Time-Saving Tip #27

When you change a habit, you change your destiny. Pick one that will enhance your life.

Once you change one habit, you now have the power to change other time habits. Dr. Ray Strand, founder of HealthyLifestyles.com, says, "If you do something for three months, you change your focus. But if you do something for fifteen months, you change your life." Turn a habit into a lasting lifestyle behavior that you can depend on.

simplify your time

It's Your Time
Change a Habit, Change Your Life (Time-Saving Habit #7)

Review your own time-saving habits and overcome the difficult ones.

Three of My Best Time Habits

1. _____
2. _____
3. _____

Three of My Time Habits to Improve

1. _____
2. _____
3. _____

Watch your thoughts; they become your words.
Watch your words; they become your actions.
Watch your actions; they become your habits.
Watch your habits; they become your character.
Watch your character, for it will become your destiny.

—Frank Outlaw

Week 2

Time-Saving Tools to Simplify Managing Your Time

This week, we will use the saved time from daily habits to invest in your time management tools. The more tools you master, the more you will be able to control your time by keeping everything together.

WEEK 2
Time-Saving Tools to Simplify Managing Your Time

Day 9	Capture More Time by Controlling Your Calendar
Day 10	Fine-Tune Your To-Do List
Day 11	Pursue a Personal Project List
Day 12	Put It All Together in a Planner System
Day 13	Practice the Power of Prioritizing
Day 14	Spruce Up Your Support Tools
Day 15	Create Weekly Time-Saving Routines

Day 9

Capture More Time
by Controlling Your Calendar

Can you change your life? Of course you can. And if you
are to simplify your life, the best place to start is with your
calendar, the place that creates the lifestyle you now live.

—Marcia Ramsland

Elaine ushered me into her office and closed the door. She began as soon as I sat down. "I used to be so organized. I had a clear desk, I returned phone calls and e-mails the same day, and I delivered projects on time. Last year I won all the top performance awards. But now I've been promoted, and I feel like my life is out of control. I can't fall asleep at night because of all the unfinished tasks. I'm also in conflict over how to balance work and my personal life. There must be a better way."

Calendar Overload

Elaine was suffering from "calendar overload," often a symptom of being a high achiever, an active volunteer, and a person struggling to keep home and work life in harmony.

She was especially anxious about having her coworkers over for an open house in two weeks. "I don't know why I agreed to it, but I am totally stressed and ready to cancel. My car needs a brake job, and my checking account is askew. I signed up for your course, Simplify Your Time, but it seemed easier to hire you to bail me out than to attend class. What can I do?"

Elaine pulled out her calendar, and out flopped multiple to-do lists, expired coupons, and a sheaf of papers for work. Embarrassed, she picked them up off the floor. "I guess I need a better filing system," she mumbled.

"OK," I began. "We need to find out how you are scheduling things at work and home."

"Frankly, I've given up writing it down. I've been much too busy. I've been out every night this week, and my house is a mess and the dishes are piled high on the kitchen counters. I haven't put away laundry in weeks, so I'm ironing clean blouses every morning before work. Where do I begin to get control?"

HELLO MY LIFE. FIX IT.

Step-by-Step Move Back into Control

I did the same thing with Elaine that I do with many of my clients: I started with her calendar. Then I suggested the following steps and walked her through them.

1. Clean up your calendar and list all the events, appointments, and due dates you know you have coming up for the next three months.
2. Fill in all the birthdays, anniversaries, and vacation days for the rest of the year.
3. Limit the number of weekend nights out to one or two on Friday, Saturday, and Sunday.
4. Balance the number of weeknights out (Monday–Thursday) to no more than two, especially if you have demanding day responsibilities.
5. Plan time in the evenings or on the weekend to catch up at home or hire housekeepers to do it for you.

Say No When Things Are Out of Control

"My number one time principle is, 'Say no when things are out of control.' That's where you are now. You need to schedule time to catch up at home and get the basics like your kitchen and laundry back together. That will take you about four hours but will immediately save thirty minutes each morning," I told Elaine. "Can you do that this evening?"

Elaine agreed but was doubtful. "How will that help my work performance?"

"Personal order is a good basis for professional excellence. Try it, and you'll see that it's true: 'When you work orderly, you think in an orderly way—all day.' And that's a great way to live."

Calendar Users Are Easier to Work With

People who use their calendars regularly are more productive and easier to work with. They include everything in their life in one place and have a sense of which days of the week work best for certain activities.

One group I was a part of worked months to put together a team retreat for ten people, carefully choosing the dates and location so the majority of interested individuals could attend. When it came down to the week before, the retreat was canceled. Why? Because the leader forgot that her son's birthday fell on one of the days. This one oversight resulted in even more time spent rescheduling the event.

All this wasted time could have been avoided if she had written in all the birthdays and anniversaries for the entire year at the beginning of the year. (But really, how could you forget your son's birthday?) When the team finally did meet, everyone decided to shop together. Those members without a planner or calendar bought one so we could literally be on the same page! Soon events were planned and scheduled, time was saved, and relationships improved.

> **Time-Saving Tip #29**
>
> Schedule your next haircut or annual physical before you leave the current appointment. Save ten minutes locating the phone number, waiting on hold, and deciding on an available date.

Get a Panoramic View of Your Month

I encourage you to commit to one monthly calendar for yourself—to hold all of your personal and professional events, dates, appointments, and so on. Train yourself to include everything there.

A monthly calendar will give you a panoramic view of your week and the weeks to come. When you preview the weekly page from Sunday through Saturday, you are doing what I call looking at time "horizontally." By spreading out your to-do list over Monday through Friday for the coming week, you can balance your week.

You can take control of your calendar by following these steps:

1. Check your calendar to see if everything is up to date, neat, and inclusive. PERSONAL   WORK = "WHITE SPACE"
2. Schedule "free choice" once or twice a week as an evening or weekend to spend as you wish—relaxing or enjoying a hobby.
3. Diagonally cross off days past this month while reflecting on whether it was time well spent.
4. Find your balance of work and personal events, and be sure to include both kinds of events on your evenings and weekends.
5. Stop the craziness by marking a big X to eliminate one commitment during a particularly busy week.
6. Circle times with friends and family that are highlights of your week.
7. Offer two time alternatives when turning down a commitment because of a prior engagement.

> **Time-Saving Tip #30**
>
> When things feel out of control, cut back on events until you are running at a reasonable pace again.

Elaine cleaned up her calendar and then counted the number of nights out per week. "Oh my. For the past ten days I have been out every night, and I have six more to go. Do you think that's too much?"

She laughed before I could reply. "I get it. If I give my time away to other people, then I have no time left for myself. I want—no, I *need*—to take back time for myself right now! I'm going to call and postpone tonight's dinner with a girlfriend and catch up on my life. That's the only way I'll be ready for the office party by Friday."

Step Up Your Personal Growth

"Elaine," I asked, "have you ever thought about using the upper margin to set some personal goals each month? That's a good way to keep your sights from getting bogged down in the mundane."

"Hmm. That sounds like more work. What do you mean?"

I showed her some examples, like these:

January
- Join a gym to get back in shape.
- Start a graduate school course.
- Put away/downscale holiday decorations.

February
- Earn As in graduate school.
- Take a winter vacation in Florida.
- Start tax return for an early refund.

> **Time-Saving Tip #31**
>
> The more you want to accomplish, the more precise you have to be with scheduling on your calendar.

I explained, "When you set three goals per month that mean something to you, your mind goes to work to achieve them. Then your personal growth is ensured even while life keeps you busy."

"I like that," said Elaine. "And I know that will keep me from getting buried in everyday life, like I used to. Right now I'll finish the month with one goal: to have a successful open house. We all need some fun, and I'll benefit by having a clean house when it's over!"

That's leveraging your time to simplify your life. Life gets complicated when you run out of time. But if you know your calendar is the basis for control, you can find your way back to fix it anytime you need to. Start with controlling your calendar, and make it work for you!

It's Your Time
Capture More Time with Your Calendar (Time Tool #1)

☐ Check your calendar to see if everything is up to date, neat, and inclusive.
☐ Diagonally cross off days that have passed this month.
☐ Schedule "free choice" once every week for the next four weeks and pencil in what you would like to do.

Avoiding the phrase "I don't have time . . ." will soon help you to realize that you do have the time needed for just about anything you choose to accomplish in life.

—Bo Bennett

simplify your time

Fine-Tune Your To-Do List

Getting closure is the feeling that something is completed.
Off your mind. Off your list. Finished. When you get closure,
you free yourself to do something which actually increases
energy. To free more energy, get more closure.

—Dru Scott Decker

Did you write a to-do list today? Most people write one for the holidays and for really busy days. Lists are the secret to getting more things accomplished in a short period of time. I was thinking about this while I listened to Claire, the mother of one of my son's soccer friends.

My busy friend slid next to me on the bench and took a deep breath. "Boy, what a day I've had," she began. "I meant to drop off my kids' books at the library on the way to school but got distracted. I made it to Starbucks and picked up a gift card for a friend's birthday, but then forgot to go next door and get more vitamins. I was right there!"

One finger at a time, Claire listed the rest of her frustrations. "I left a finished report for work sitting on my kitchen counter, a five-dollar restaurant coupon for lunch inside the folder, and an important check to deposit in my other purse."

She sighed yet turned to me with a smile. "But I'm here now and ready to relax. Oh, wait! I just remembered our car insurance is due tomorrow. I'll have to send it overnight. Why am I always so busy yet accomplishing so little?"

Claire's To-Do List

I shared with Claire one of the keys I teach my clients: *create a detailed to-do list of items you want to accomplish.* Writing things down supports our memory and points us toward satisfaction at the end of the day.

Claire pulled out a sheet of paper. "Here. Show me how that works." In just one minute, we listed all the items she had forgotten that day. Now she had a template to use each night for smoother days and less stress.

Diagram 10A

CLAIRE'S TO-DO LIST

Wednesday, September 23		
To-Dos on the Way to School/Work	**Take:**	
1. ✓ Drop off books at library.	1. ✓ Library books	
2. ✓ Get Jenny to school by 7:40 a.m.	2. __ Work file folder	
3. ✓ Get Starbucks gift card.	3. __ Check for bank	
4. Get more vitamins.	4. __ $5 lunch coupon	
5. Mail insurance forms.	5. __ Insurance forms	

Claire did remember to get to the library and Starbucks before work, but she lost a lot of time catching up on things she forgot. A daily to-do list would help her, especially if she wrote down what she needed to take as she listed her to-dos and checked them off before leaving home.

simplify your time

Can a To-Do List Help Me?

Put simply, a to-do list is a list of actions you want to remember or need to accomplish in a given day or short time period. It solves the problem of "I forgot . . ." and relieves the worry that you won't remember an item that comes up during the day.

My friend Liz once said, "My mind is like a computer, and I've run out of RAM [memory space]. And like a computer, I think my brain is about to crash." I heard recently that our short-term memory can only hold seven items before it starts pushing things out. That's why we forget details that we intended to handle.

One way to manage our time is to control the way events occur, preferably by planning what's coming instead of losing time over forgotten tasks.

What Do I Do with the List Each Night?

At the end of the day, evaluate your to-do list by noting what you did well, how you can complete what didn't happen, and what you can cross off the list as unnecessary, after all. You will finish more things when you rely on paper rather than memory.

Congratulate yourself on the goals you reached, and plan your list for the following day. As you practice this habit, I guarantee you will see results. But you must promise to cross off low-priority items or delegate them to another person or another day when you feel overwhelmed.

Remember, your to-do list should work for you, not against you. You decide what to put on it. Don't let it control your life. Just change the list if it is too much.

My Order, Time Order, or Priority Order?

When you start listing items on your to-do list, you have three choices: you can put to-dos in the order they occur to you, in the time order in which you will complete them. As you build one style you will become more skilled at getting the right things completed at the right time.

(handwritten note: ✗ CALENDAR OF ASSUMPTIONS)

Diagram 10B

CLAIRE'S PLANNER PAGE

	TIME EVENTS	TO DO
		3 PRIORITY PROJECTS:
7:00	☐ Library	**A1** ☐ Work/kids/school/ errands—gift card/vitamins
8:00	☐ Starbucks gift card	**A2** ☐ Return library books
	☐ Vitamins	
9:00		**A3** ☐ Mail insurance forms
10:00	**8–3 WORK**	
11:00		
Noon	Luncheon	
1:00	☐ Birthday gift and card	**CALLS:** ☐ RSVP Sat. dinner
2:00		☐ Babysitter for Sat.
3:00	☐ Pick up dry cleaning	
	☐ Put away laundry	
4:00	**4–5 Soccer**	
5:00		**AT HOME TO DO:**
	5:30 Dinner	☐ Put away laundry
6:00	**FREE CHOICE**	
7:00		
		DISCUSS WITH SPOUSE:
8:00		☐ Weekend plans
	☐ Downtime to relax	
9:00	☐ Plan tommorrow on paper	

Fill in the Night Before:

1. TIME EVENTS
2. CALLS
3. ERRANDS
4. PRIORITY PROJECTS

Take for the Day:

☐ Library books (5)
☐ Work file
☐ Check for bank
☐ Lunch coupon
☐ Insurance forms

*Make it a habit to place these items in one "launch" spot the night before. Take along each morning.

Ten Reminders for a Successful To-Do List

1. **Limit it.** Find out how many items you can handle in a day. When my kids were in school, I did nine items; but when they were home, I could only do three. Find the number that works for you.

2. **Write it.** Each day, write down what you need to accomplish. Clear out mental clutter by putting it on paper. Leave a space between each item to sandwich in higher priorities.

3. **Verb-alize it.** Begin each to-do item with an action verb (e.g., pay bills, call Mary, send birthday card, put away laundry, outline proposal, etc.). Your mind visualizes you in action as you "verb-alize" it and then write it down.

I LIKE IT!

4. **Post it.** Keep your to-do list in the same place each day. Whether it's in your planner, on your kitchen counter, or on a sticky note on your computer monitor, keep it anchored in one spot.

5. **Refer to it.** Refer to your list throughout the day until you are finished. Consider it your personal compass pointing you in the right direction.

6. **Adjust it.** Plan your morning to-dos the night before. Before lunch each day, plan your afternoon list.

7. **Check it off.** As you complete each item, check it off with a red pen, cross it off, or delete it from your computer list.

8. **Practice it.** It takes practice to create a list that works one day at a time. Avoid making this a long-term project list. Keep it short and use it to focus on daily tasks only.

9. **Evaluate it.** At the end of every day, see what worked and what didn't. Then make a mental (or diary) note to keep what worked and what didn't. This will help you avoid making the same mistake twice.

10. **Toss it!** When the list is complete, toss it! Enjoy two great results: emotional relief and a clear mind.

> **Time-Saving Tip #34**
>
> A written to-do list is the secret to clearing your mind of mental clutter and accomplishing more each day.

> **Time-Saving Tip #35**
>
> A to-do list is like the wrapper on a fast-food meal. Once it serves its purpose, throw it out.

A to-do list is the most basic yet most powerful time management tool to correspond with your monthly calendar. By using a to-do list, you will gain a reputation for getting things finished and peace of mind that everything is accounted for in a day.

It's Your Time
Fine-Tune Your To-Do List (Time Tool #2)

☐ Decide the best format for writing a daily to-do list and stick to it.
☐ Keep it in one place and refer to it all day long.
☐ Use it every day for a month and see how it improves your life.

You have to rewrite and update your list from time to time. . . . If you find you are recopying whole pages frequently, it is a sign that you're trying to do way too much or keeping too much detail on your list. The list should be brief.

—Porter Knight

Day 11

Pursue a Personal Project List

If setting deadlines for yourself has never worked before, it's because you kept those dates in your head (or your pocket calendar, where you never look six months ahead). In your head there is no time! In your head it is always now.

—Barbara Sher

Have you noticed how some items keep cropping up on your to-do list, but you never start them? Chances are they're not the kind of to-dos that can be completed in one day. They require more time and attention. So put them on a project list.

The two lists are practically cousins. One supports the other. A to-do list covers daily action steps. A project list includes larger tasks that take more time and steps. Both help you focus your time and attention on things you need or want to do and will benefit from doing.

But I Already Have Project Lists!

Diane was in my audience when we talked about project lists. She was excited to share a personal victory. "I'm a teacher, and I save all my projects for the summer. Last summer, I wrote a two-page list on a legal pad and posted it on the back door. I looked at it every day and felt so organized."

I admired her enthusiasm. "So how did it go?" I asked. "Did you complete some significant projects?" I expected to hear about organized closets, the family room redecorated, paper piles filed, and afternoons as a family spent at the pool once the morning work was finished.

But Diane looked a bit sheepish. "Well, actually . . . I didn't do any of them. It just felt good to have them listed," she concluded. "I suppose that's not enough, right?"

To help Diane get on track with her projects, I shared with her three important things about project lists:

1. **Put no more than ten items on your project list.** Don't add another one until you complete one or cross it off.
2. **Assign each project a beginning and ending time on your calendar.** Half the battle is starting, and the other half is working through to completion. Keep your momentum going by regularly including a small to medium project as part of your lifestyle.
3. **Decide if this is a short monthly or longer seasonal project.** A monthly project can be written in the top margin of your monthly calendar. Generally, you can accomplish three projects per month for home or work if you stay focused and look for pockets of time to work on them. A seasonal project is categorized as fall, winter, spring, or summer. Post or tape the name of the project to a spot you see each day, such as your computer monitor, bathroom mirror, or kitchen bulletin board.

Diane's Seasonal Project List

"Oh, I see," said Diane. "I need to limit my list, pick a time frame, and then start on projects that are small and manageable."

"That's right," I replied. "We're more likely to finish things that are divided into small pieces. If they're too big, we procrastinate and never start." I gave her an example of what her list could look like for the summer:

simplify your time

- Put kids' papers in a memory book.
- Clean up my desk.
- Decorate my "blah" bedroom.

Diane laughed at decorating her "blah" bedroom. "It has an old bedspread I never liked. I'm going to replace it, paint the room, and hang some new pictures. Mornings are hard enough without waking up to a depressing room." And she agreed, "Putting away my kids' papers and mine would be a great way to start the summer. What a lift it would give to do even one decorating project a year."

STEP 1: PICK YOUR PROJECTS FOR THE YEAR

What changes would you like to make in your life? Check off the boxes below that interest you, or add your own projects.

	Fall	Winter	Spring	Summer
Organize photo books	___	___	___	___
Clean the garage	___	___	___	___
Update my résumé	___	___	___	___
Put in a closet system	___	___	___	___
Paint the master bedroom	___	___	___	___
Do more scrapbooking	___	___	___	___
Do my gardening	___	___	___	___
Finish quilts for grandkids	___	___	___	___
Take a computer course	___	___	___	___
Clean out my files	___	___	___	___
Start a book club	___	___	___	___
Learn to snow ski	___	___	___	___
Open a 401k	___	___	___	___
Shampoo the carpets	___	___	___	___
_____	___	___	___	___
_____	___	___	___	___

It's usually best to add items that you can envision yourself doing in the near future that will either make an area beautiful or make your day-to-day life easier.

STEP 2: MARK THE APPROPRIATE SEASON FOR EACH PROJECT

Most people make a project list—and want everything done by the end of next weekend! Since your time is already full, find projects that are motivating enough for you to redirect your time and energy over a month or a quarter. Then go back to the list and mark which season best fits each project. For example:

Fall: Start a project—take a self-improvement course, create a scrapbook to share at the holidays, make craft projects for Christmas gifts, update financial plans.

Winter: Inside projects—organize photo books, clean out files, take a computer course.

Spring: Outside projects—take a spring break vacation, clean the garage, shampoo the carpets, plant your garden.

Summer: Light projects—update your résumé, repair the grandfather clock, be outside, vacation with family and friends, paint and decorate a bedroom.

STEP 3: SEQUENCE THE PROJECTS INTO A SEASONAL TIMELINE

Post a timeline (such as this one) where you will see it regularly. Once you set a target and a date, you will start noticing things that will help you make it happen.

WINTER	SPRING	SUMMER	FALL
Organize DVDs and CDs (January–February)	Plant the garden and clean the yard and garage (April–May)	Paint and decorate my bedroom (July–August)	Start a new class (September–October)

Start a file or two-pocket folder for each project, and keep adding ideas as they come up. When you approach your season to begin, create an action plan in a list of sequential steps taped to the front cover of the folder. Set a start date and the time allowed, and coordinate the timeline with your calendar. Leverage it before an event or holiday, but allow three weeks' leeway to finish up.

How Does Tackling a Project Simplify My Time?

Sometimes it might feel like a better use of your time to do nothing. Why rock the boat? At times, this can be a wise choice. On the other hand, taking action can bring peace and order. After all, if you have to view a messy space or an undecorated room each day, you will develop "visual tuneout" and never notice it . . . until the day the Realtor makes you fix it so you can sell your home. Do it now, and enjoy the results while you live there.

During a radio show on which I was the guest, one caller had a challenging scenario. Lilly was a frazzled mother of two high-energy preschoolers who needed her constant attention. She lamented, "When will I have time to get my photos into albums? And I have all these boxes of old papers that I have to go through."

Generally, I suggest people list projects by season, but in her case I had a different suggestion. "Simply label the photos with the year and grade level of the children, place the newest ones in front, and put them in a labeled decorative photo box. When it's the right time, perhaps when the kids are in grade school, you'll be able to get the photos in books for each of their birthdays. After that, they will be easier to maintain."

Lilly, like so many people I've spoken with, let out a sigh of relief. She realized that she didn't need to pressure herself beyond what she was able. All she needed to do was to label the year and topic on the outside of the well-ordered photo boxes. Even a small temporary step can simplify your time.

Time-Saving Tip #37

Finish a project by linking it to an event or holiday when you will show it off to company. Peer pressure works wonders.

IN PENCIL ON THE BACK IN A CORNER

Time-Saving Tip #38

Finish a project and savor the results. You will simplify your life, move ahead, and develop the skill of perseverance—something you can't learn any other way.

The Rewards of Projects

Lisa, a working single gal in her twenties, decided that during her one-week vacation between Christmas and New Year's, she would go through all ten boxes of her school papers and sort them. Next she would redecorate her room, replacing her childhood decorations with those of a young professional.

ASSEMBLED A TEAM + DELEGATED TASKS

While Lisa sorted from morning to night, her dad painted the high ceiling and walls and moved furniture with her brother. She and her mom gathered decorating tips from Ethan Allen. Lisa was able to complete all this in her ten-day time span.

When she returned to work, Lisa discovered that her professional life picked up when she put her personal space in order. People sensed she was in control, and they respected her for it. The same can be true for you.

It's Your Time
Pursue a Personal Project List (Time Tool #3)

☐ Finish a project to show you can do it!
☐ Find a partner or mentor to guide you through the next project.
☐ Start a project that you can successfully complete soon.

The secret of getting ahead is getting started.
The secret of getting started is breaking your complex
overwhelming tasks into small manageable tasks,
and then starting on the first one.

—Mark Twain

simplify your time

Put It All Together in a Planner System

Improve your business, your life, your relationships,
your finances, and your health. When you do, the
whole world improves.

—Mark Victor Hansen

"Marcia, I've got to tell you—you have changed my life by telling me to get a planner to hold my calendar, to-do list, and project lists!"

It was 8:00 a.m., and six of us were lounging around a table drinking coffee. We had arrived at the motel the previous night, stayed up late on our team retreat, and were ready for a morning walk on the beach.

Lynn continued, "I write my to-do list in there, our home projects are planned with my husband for the next six months, and I feel like I have so much more time."

"What planner?" Debbie asked.

Lynn pulled out her small, black ring binder and started showing the others the pages. "It has all the months for this year, daily pages for this month, phone numbers . . ." She looked around the table. "Don't you gals have one?"

"No," came the reply from around the table. One woman admitted, "I used to have one, but it never worked."

They peppered me with questions about where to get a planner and how to use it after seeing all of Lynn's neat entries. I was a bit embarrassed about being put on the spot so early in the morning. After a few minutes of discussion, they turned to me and declared unanimously, "Let's skip the beach walk and get to the store—now!" It was the first time I had ever seen anyone skip a walk on the beach for a trip to the office supply store.

Getting It All Together

In my experience, the number one time problem is not too much to do, nor is it too little time to do it. It's the feeling of being fragmented with too many things pulling us apart. Our mind works overtime trying to remember everything we have to do, want to do, and need to do.

COMMON EXAMPLE OF HOW WE GET OFF TRACK

The problem arises when our calendar is at home while we are at the dentist and need to schedule an appointment. Or when we are out on an errand and have time to do one more errand but can't remember what's on our list. And it's really compounded when we want to schedule next year's spring vacation but we don't know if Easter is in March or April without next year's calendar handy.

What's the Answer?

The answer is to find a time system that works smoothly for your current needs. Eventually you may need to progress to the next level time system. When something isn't working, that may mean you should get a new system in January or September. But don't just buy a new monthly wall calendar. Your life has very likely moved beyond the monthly calendar with its one-inch squares for each day.

Four Time Management Systems

Most people operate in one of four time management systems. From the basic to the more complex, they are:

1. THE CRISIS AND MEMORY METHOD. This method reacts to urgent items and relies on memory, two things that usually don't work well together under pressure. It is reactive, not proactive, and mostly done from memory. The results can range from a restful to stressful lifestyle depending on how many things the person has to respond to.

2. THE LIST AND PILE METHOD. This system relies on visual reminders such as items laid out on counters—plus lists, schedules, and appointment cards plastered to the refrigerator or desktop. This visual system works when there are one to three items, but it falls apart when the lists and piles turn into a sea of clutter.

3. THE CALENDAR METHOD. The monthly calendar hanging on the wall or a desk blotter on the desktop is fine if you want to know what day it is. Beyond that, any kind of list floats from desk to car to the top of a pile and can easily get lost. A monthly calendar enables you to meet your appointments, but reminders are generally littered on sticky notes around your computer monitor.

4. THE PLANNER METHOD. A planner is a book with sections to include your calendar, to-do list, project list, and phone numbers all in one spot. It can be either a hard copy that you write in or an electronic PDA (personal digital assistant) or Blackberry linked to your computer. Everything is included in this one spot, and your tasks are linked to a day and time.

> **Time-Saving Tip #40**
>
> Plan on a two-month learning curve when you change to a new planner or PDA. You will save an estimated one hour a week once you have all your lists and tools in one place.

What Do I Need?

When I work with clients, I like to see what they are using for a calendar and a daily to-do list. And I like to see if they have a project list (or goals) for any time in the future. The people who have all three are the ones who value their time enough to manage it well.

Put It All Together in One System

As we arrived at the office supply store, I briefly described the five elements of a working time system, either on paper or in digital format:

1. CHOOSE A COVER YOU LIKE. Planners are available in department stores or office supply stores in attractive binders in various sizes and customized sections and pages you need. PDAs also have many storage options, including small binders with notepads and organizers with a slot for your PDA and checkbook and credit cards. Choose one or the other and then add the next sections.

2. CHOOSE A MONTHLY CALENDAR. Carefully choose a calendar with tabs on the edges, noting each month, one with page colors that are appealing to you. For the most room to write things, choose a calendar with two pages for each month. In a PDA, you have calendars for years ahead in one tiny machine to navigate with just a click of the mouse.

3. CHOOSE THE SECTION IN WHICH TO WRITE YOUR DAILY TIME PLAN AND TO-DOS. That will either be one page per day, two pages per day, or a week at a glance. The more you want to accomplish, the more room you need. In a PDA, all these systems are available plus tracking to check off and color-code tasks, such as those that require travel, those that are business or family related, and so on. The benefit of a PDA is the extremely large amount of information you can have at your fingertips.

4. CHOOSE TABS AND LINED PAGES FOR YOUR ROLES. This will allow you to have a section for your work, home projects, a home-based business, and general information. Keep brief notes here. Most PDAs sync right into your personal computer, so your notes can be extensive and you can access information on your computer as well.

5. CHOOSE A PHONE AND ADDRESS SECTION THAT YOU CAN CUSTOMIZE. You can keep store hours, directions to a client, phone numbers, and passwords here. A PDA has a contact book, and your PDA can dial numbers as your phone.

Shopping Is Fun!

The six of us shopped like we were at Nordstrom choosing a purse with five other girlfriends. "Look at this!" "I like this one." "What do you think of this color?" Everyone chose something different: Debbie got a medium-sized black planner, her mother got a smaller portable red one, and the other Debi couldn't find anything she liked.

We carpooled from the office supply store to Barnes & Noble, and there Debi found an executive-looking planner that laid flat, but wasn't quite right. "Don't settle for something 'almost' right," I cautioned. "Keep looking this week until you find it."

Marianne decided she would pull out her old planner at home. It was five years old, so she tossed the old pages and got the new ones online from Daytimer. She was ecstatic to get organized again.

A week later I saw Debi, and she was beaming with her new planner. "I kept looking and found one I love. Now I can see what I have to do and I'm not wasting time any-more. I have a full life!"

At our next monthly meeting, they all reported that they had projects and plans in "real time" on dates and months. No more scattered to-do lists and project lists that amounted to half-finished good intentions!

> ## Time-Saving Tip #41
>
> Visit an office supply store or search online to find a planner system that will consolidate your time management tools.

What Do You Depend On for Accomplishing Things?

CONSOLIDATE! "LESS IS MORE"

By being able to pull together your many activities in one spot, you will gain control of your time. When you miss deadlines, feel stuck in a rut, or wish you were doing something else, consider changing your planning system.

Personally, I love to see people progress from a monthly wall calendar to something more complete. My favorite is the hard copy planner. My motto for using one is, "If you can't fit it all on one page, you can't live it in one day." ← ✗✗✗ That's the value of planning your time on paper.

However, my friend and best-selling author Pam Farrel gave up her paper organizer years ago. She says, "When you move at a fast pace, have to plan two to five years out, and go to meetings where vital information is needed in moments so a decision can be made, the two tools you will need are a PDA that doubles as your cell phone and a good laptop. With these tools, I not only keep track of what I need to do, but I can program reminders with alarms so that I don't have to remember all the details. I can also have my family's or coworkers' schedules on hand in my system, which is handy for scheduling meetings and keeping track of our busy family's multiple activities."

Pull together your calendar, your lists, and your goals in one time management system so time will flow more smoothly through your day. You will wonder how you ever managed time without it.

BABY STEPS: I WILL GRADUATE TO A
PDA/CELL PHONE → LAPTOP SYNCH-UP

It's Your Time
Put It All Together in a Planner (Time Tool #4)

☐ At the soonest opportunity, get a planner or the missing components to your time system mentioned. Start fresh!

☐ Be more purposeful about the time tool you use, and jot down your plans every evening or first thing in the morning. You will be more productive with a well-planned day than one that is left to chance.

If you want to know what day it is, any calendar will do.
But if you want to gain control of your time, schedule
priority tasks, and gain a reputation for getting
things done, use a planner!

—Harold Taylor

simplify your time

Practice the Power of Prioritizing

In my experience, when people do more planning,
more informally and naturally, they relieve a great
deal of stress and obtain better results.

—David Allen

Dan swung around in his office chair when he heard me enter. He smiled and waved me in as he wrapped up his phone conversation. "OK. I have to go," he concluded. "My professional organizer is here, and she's going to get me organized. Don't laugh. I'm really going to do it this time. You just wait—I'll be a changed man." With that, he hung up the phone.

"Boy, am I glad to see you," he told me. "I've got at least ten projects to complete before I leave for my next trip. Do you think I'll be ready day after tomorrow?"

I took note of the sea of papers on the desktop. I also noticed two briefcases on the floor and a credenza and conference table full of stacks of paper. I almost said yes—and then I noticed three boxes of paper under his desk with as much order as a recycle bin. I asked what they were doing there.

Dan appeared sheepish. "They're the papers I put away when I knew you were coming. It's my way of cleaning up my desk."

We both laughed. I shook my head and smiled. "I have a hunch it's a matter of prioritizing. And from the looks of things, you need that skill. Let's get going."

Prioritizing Accomplishes More in Less Time

Setting priorities is one of the higher-level skills necessary for simplifying your time. To get started, ask yourself two questions:

1. What am I going to do first?
2. How many things do I plan to accomplish in the time available?

I asked Dan if he cooked. He responded, "No, but I like to eat."

I suggested we look at his priorities in the same way a chef looks at preparing a meal. For example, if a chef were serving a lasagna dinner with Caesar salad and French bread with melted butter, he'd put the lasagna in the oven first, toss the salad while the dish is baking, and then add the French bread at the last moment so everything gets finished at the right time in the right order.

Prioritizing Under Pressure

I suggested that Dan use that model to look at what he had to do to prepare for his trip. He came up with the following list:

- Bring closure to everything before leaving for overseas for ten days, including e-mail responses, paper projects, and phone calls.
- Prepare for the trip by confirming final details with the other team members and packing my work-related paperwork and personal belongings.
- Delegate work for my new assistant to do while I'm away, such as handling the boxes under my desk.

As much as Dan had to do, and as challenging as it would be to finish so much in such a short time, I knew we had one big factor on our side: people are most productive right before a trip. Tasks that would have taken weeks for us to do otherwise we would now finish in short order. Time pressures make some people more decisive, and I had a feeling Dan was one of them.

Prioritize According to Important and Urgent

In a time crunch moment, you need to do the urgent *and* important. For Dan, that meant confirming flights, packing paperwork for the trip, and leaving contact numbers and instructions for emergencies.

Delegate the Checklist

To maximize your time, delegate the list to an assistant or family member who can take care of it while you move to the next priority. Save your time for what you do best. If there is no one to delegate the list to, do it at a low-energy time like midafternoon. Stick to the task, time the procedure, and list the time frame on the checklist to refer to next time.

Make a List of the Top Five Items

Our short-term memory can hold only a limited number of items at a time. So I asked Dan to focus his activities by listing the top five things that come to mind. He rattled off his mental list while I jotted the items down:

1. Call travel agent and find out where the airline tickets are.
2. E-mail the team and tell them the details of the trip.
3. Prepare my speeches and PowerPoint presentations for the trip.
4. Give assistant a list of things to do while I am gone.
5. Wrap up phone calls and e-mails.

Deadlines Create a Need for Decisions and Closure

Dan discovered, as most of us do, that no matter how much we prepare for a trip, there are last-minute things to do. Keep a reusable checklist for the three days before any trip to minimize that stress. Going from memory is the most stressful thing you can do.

Dan decided to pull together his PowerPoint and first of three speeches while he kept a pad of paper handy with three columns: Assistant To-Dos, Phone Calls, and E-mails.

A Personal Turning Point

Dan now had to decide whether he would focus on his speeches or spend the time getting things in order for his assistant. It all boiled down to time choices.

After we talked, he chose to focus his time among the three items, doing first the item that required the highest concentration. He limited speech writing to one-third of his time and moved on to his three-column list.

Dan was catching on. With this new bit of information, Dan divided up the remaining 1.5 hours before departure to a half hour on his first speech, a half hour on pulling together action items to leave for his assistant, and a half hour returning calls and e-mails, picking out the highest priorities.

> **Time-Saving Tip #43**
>
> Write a checklist of action steps in ten minutes and save thirty minutes of helter-skelter activity as you get ready for a trip, a regular meeting, or an important presentation.

The "One Thing" Principle

The "one thing" principle is simply this: *sometimes there is only enough time to do one thing.* At such times, focus on the urgent and postpone the rest of your activities. Although postponed activities can create trouble, there are times when it's a risk worth taking.

When your priorities are not clear to you, try finishing this statement regarding those items that need attention: "If I could only do one thing, I would . . ." Then write down that action step and put a number by it. Then ask yourself the same question for #2, #3, and so on until you have assigned each task a priority number.

For example:

1. ___ Call the travel agent.
3. ___ E-mail the team.
2. ___ Pull together my PowerPoints and speech.
5. ___ Assign my assistant work.
4. ___ Return critical phone calls and e-mails.

Remember, you always have time for the things you do first. Just make sure you divide your time to include the remaining priorities as well.

Be proactive about prioritizing your to-do list first thing in the morning so you can be productive the rest of the day. It takes a disciplined person to act on difficult items early in the day. Once you do so, however, you will yield a high return on your investment.

Time-Saving Tip #44

The more you prioritize, the better you will become at gauging how much you can accomplish. Prioritizing is the best way to sort and simplify a long list.

It's Your Time
Practice the Power of Prioritizing (Time Tool #5)

☐ Always prioritize your to-do list with numbers, especially the top three items.

☐ Divide your available time to complete the tasks and keep moving forward.

☐ Prioritize by asking the relief question: "What one task would give me the most relief it I got it out of the way?" Complete that task first.

When you get right down to the root of the meaning of the word *succeed*, you find it simply means to follow through.

—F. W. Nichol

Spruce Up Your Support Tools

People love to win. If you're not totally clear about the purpose of what you're doing, you have no chance of winning.

—David Allen

Dan's assistant, Kelly, was relieved to hear her boss was getting help to organize his office. She was organized and couldn't understand the disarray of paper everywhere. "How can Dan get anything done?" she mused aloud. "It would drive me nuts."

"He seems to have his own system," I replied. "But I agree that as president his style could potentially limit the growth of the organization." Then I told Kelly, "You could help him. Men and women gravitate toward leaders, but if leaders can't run things well, people get disillusioned and drift away. It's like the slogan says, 'The speed of the leader determines the rate of the pack.'"

Later that day, Dan mentioned he stopped at home on his lunch hour to pick up some papers he needed for a trip. As he walked into the kitchen, he heard the squeals of his little children. He looked around and wondered why his wife couldn't get all the clutter under control. *Oh well,* he thought. *She's a good mom. Who am I to change her?*

Finding Your Key Support Tools

Everyone has systems—but are they working well? That's a question we all need to ask ourselves. Dan and his wife could benefit from some key tools that would help them stay organized to have more free time to meet career and family goals.

For work, there are many tools to choose from: file folders, three-ring binders, computer systems, and even flat surfaces on the desktop. Each one can save you time if you make wise use of it.

For home, there are cabinets, shelves, drawers, and bookcases to help you organize everything from spices, books, and CDs to daily mail and paperwork. If you use them well, you will have more time to relax.

What's the Simple Solution?

Simplify the steps from point A of using an item to point B of retrieving it again, and you'll automatically cut in half the time spent doing that task.

SEVEN KEY SUPPORT TOOLS AT WORK		
Support Tool	**Why and When?**	**Time Saved**
1. File Folders: Keep new folders and a label maker within reach to label a file when you have eight or more related papers.	File folders help you eliminate paper clutter as soon as it crosses your desk.	Using file folders saves five to twenty minutes each day spent looking for a specific paper.
2. File Drawer: One file drawer should contain your current work, which is listed on your to-do and project lists.	Current projects can get lost unless you have a place to file them each day.	Cleaning up your desk at night can save you thirty minutes of start-up time.

3.	Three-Ring Binders: Good for storing papers and projects you refer to regularly. Buy tabbed dividers to sort papers.	Numerous printed papers get lost on a desktop. A labeled binder is easier to find and use if you include like items.	Save up to fifteen minutes by referring to agendas and newsletters you write and refer to.
4.	Flat Surfaces: Keep your to-do list, day's work, phone list, and blank pad in the same spot.	Tools that are in the same place each day are ready to use. Put things away each day.	Eliminate five to ten minutes of stress each day by keeping desk items in the same place.
5.	Contact Management System: ACT or Microsoft Outlook neatly holds contact info and notes. Record weekly.	Having one system minimizes scraps of paper, business cards, and brochures.	Invest five minutes typing to save five minutes searching per item.
6.	Computer Files: Consistently label similar files with name and date.	Poorly labeled computer files cost valuable time searching. Delete daily or archive files monthly.	Computer files labeled systematically save five to fifteen minutes of search time.
7.	System Log: Keep a record chart of progress listing start and finish dates and other pertinent information.	This "go-to" sheet keeps repeat tasks organized. Create a system for weekly review.	A system log can save ten minutes or more of start-up and finish time if you record regularly.

Putting These Tools into Practice

After showing Kelly the value of these tools and the time she and Dan could save, Kelly was smiling. "This is great," she said. "I do these things automatically." She looked toward the door. "Here comes Dan, so we can start."

Time-Saving Tip #45

Create a file folder for every topic that has a minimum of eight related pieces of paper. Result? Save five minutes every time you look for a specific piece of paper on that subject.

Time-Saving Tip #46

Use one corner of your desk to stair-step your work in order of priority. Save ten minutes of sorting time for each project that day.

Together the three of us sorted the desktop and put the tools to work. Each of us found loose papers that needed a new file folder to keep them together. And we removed half of a file drawer of old files to make room for current ones. Dan was amazed at how much he had been holding on to. Some folders were dated five years earlier. He stood over the recycle bin, tossing at a fast clip.

Meanwhile, Kelly put staff meeting agendas and important magazine articles into three-ring binders with sheet protectors. Phone numbers and business cards were gathered from the nooks and crannies around the phone and in-box. These went into a file for Kelly to log in later.

The greatest asset, however, was listing the unfinished work on two log sheets: one for Dan and one for Kelly. They followed up by checking in with each other on Monday, Wednesday, and Friday mornings to review their progress.

Use Your Desk as an Organizing Tool

Dan put his papers in stair-step order on the left side of his desk. The highest priority was on the top, the second one under and one inch behind it, and so on.

Kelly had a spotless desk with eight single sheets of paper laid out. She knew the upper left of her desk was her highest priority. The papers then moved toward the right in diminishing priorities. She accomplished more than most people because she moved across the desk from one task to the next in an orderly way.

What About Tools for Home?

Dan's wife, Lori, stopped in as we finished up. "Wow, how did you do it? I'd love for our home to look like this."

Dan hugged his wife and winked at me. "What systems do we need? I promise I'll help this time."

Together, we listed tools they could use at home.

FIVE KEY SUPPORT TOOLS AT HOME		
Support Tool	**Why and When?**	**Time Saved**
1. Mail System: Process mail in the kitchen with five file folders: Calendar, To Do, To Decide, Information, My Interests.	Mail clutter wastes time and space. Respond to each piece before dinner or all on the weekend.	Save ten minutes each day or an hour on the weekend by processing your mail daily.
2. Magazine System: Keep publications on a certain end table or in a magazine holder.	They will become floating clutter if you're not careful. Read and replace the prior issue.	Save thirty minutes of skimming through the same magazine by replacing it.
3. Photo System: Label and file photos in a box the day you get them, newest in the front. Label digital photos by topic and date.	Photo clutter will keep you from enjoying your photos. Label and file them right away.	Save hours, even days of sorting by keeping up with your photo files or albums.
4. Cabinet Systems: Alphabetize similar-sized spices and canned goods with labels forward.	Organize items on shelves by category when you put groceries away.	Save five critical minutes before meals by having pantry items in order.
5. Cleanup Systems: Pick up the family room, bedrooms, and other clutter spots daily.	Daily clutter can be overwhelming. Pick up rooms before leaving them or before dinner.	Save fifteen stressful minutes in the evening trying to catch up on the day's activities.

How Long Does Change Take?

I'd like to report that everything changed for Dan and Lori and Kelly right away. But we all know that lasting change takes time to achieve. It takes twenty-one times to create a habit! All three of them could see the value of an organized team at work and an organized family at home.

It's Your Time
Spruce Up Your Support Tools (Time Tool #6)

☐ Solve time and paper-flow problems at work and home by creating a new system.

☐ Keep papers and notebooks in the same places.

☐ Get something new at an office supply store to simplify a messy area.

When you are making a success of something,
it's not work, it's a way of life.

—Andy Granatelli

Create Weekly Time-Saving Routines

Life is a journey, a process. Every day you must deliberately make the effort to take a few steps. Learn, grow, become better than you are today. The secret of your future is hidden in your daily routine.

—John Maxwell

Have you ever heard the saying, "We always have time for what we want to do"? I disagree. We don't always have time for the things we want to do. We work hard, we help others, we meet professional deadlines, we push ourselves to get things in order for our family, and we say, "Yes, I'll drive the carpool tonight," even when we are exhausted ourselves.

But when do we have time for personal tasks that are just for us—at work and at home? One way is to make time by creating time-saving routines.

Successful People Practice Successful Routines

I can imagine what you're thinking when you see the word *routine*—boring, regular, no fun. But what if creating a routine included a well-groomed

Time-Saving Tip #48

. . . .

Include personal
grooming tasks such
as a manicure or facial
masque on regular
days of the week so
you can depend on
looking good every day.

appearance, a spotless home, today's work completed when you leave the office, and dinner a breeze to prepare?

Successful people don't leave things to chance or impulse. They depend on good routines, and so can you. Never fear when your workload gets heavy and company drops by unexpectedly. You'll be ready if you have routines that work for you.

A weekly routine can include simple tasks such as regularly taking out the trash the day before garbage pickup and assigning a regular day for grocery shopping. To get started, think of areas of your life that are cluttered or routine tasks that have hit-or-miss success. Then create a customized system for personal use, for work routines, or for home maintenance. Create a chart when you become aware of tasks falling through the cracks—those items that would enhance your life if you kept up with them.

Weekly Personal Routines

Sue always felt rushed getting ready for the day, but she realized the real problem was the time she wasted while doing so. "I have nothing to wear," she lamented. "The clean laundry is still in the basket, and I can't seem to get a coordinated outfit together in short order." But she didn't want to spend her valuable weekends cleaning and arranging her closet.

We created a routine chart for her personal area that kept everything put away and weeded out. It took the mad dash out of her mornings, and Sue later reported it felt good to walk calmly out the door. Her self-confidence in other areas grew as well.

WEEKLY PERSONAL ROUTINE

Monday	Wash and put laundry away the same day.
Tuesday	Organize one category (e.g., shirts or slacks).
Wednesday	Empty trash cans.

Thursday	Clean the sink and mirror.
Friday	Reorganize one shelf or drawer.
Saturday	Put away dresser clutter.
Sunday	Enjoy clean personal space.

Sue taped this schedule inside her bathroom mirror cabinet and made the five-to-ten-minute daily task part of her morning dressing time. She kept at it, and in a few weeks she was caught up with her closet organization. After that, she hardly ever spent her weekends cleaning up her bedroom.

Weekly Work Routines

Mandy rarely met her work deadlines. She often e-mailed the agenda for the weekly staff meeting only a half hour before everyone met. The meeting slipped by week after week, and the morale of her team was sliding downhill as well. "We used to be so productive," she mused aloud.

Mandy took a look at what she once did with skill and ease and what she needed to do now. She made an important change by taping a reminder chart by her calendar for each day of the week.

WEEKLY WORK ROUTINE

Monday	Compile sales for previous week/month. Send report.
Tuesday	E-mail staff agenda for tomorrow. Prepare today.
Wednesday	Follow up on sales meeting. Generate new business.
Thursday	Take client or staff to lunch. Work on relationships.
Friday	Confirm client appointments for next week.

With routine tasks listed by days, Mandy became productive and received more support from her staff. She hoped it would result in praise—and a raise—

Time-Saving Tip #49

· · · · · · · · · · · · · · · · · · · ·

List five things you do
each week for your
job, and assign each
one to a day of the
week. Pencil a dot
after it every time you
complete it on the
intended day.

at her next job review. She began to take charge again and was eager to accomplish the day's tasks no matter how others responded.

Weekly Home Routines

Jackie and Bill decided they didn't like letting grocery shopping, laundry, yard work, and errands fill every Saturday. So they developed a system that allowed them to get the errands out of the way during the week, leaving more time for golf or snow skiing on the weekends.

They listed what they needed to do on a regular basis and what they preferred to do during their free time now that their kids were grown. They created their list over the course of the week and posted it beside the calendar to refer to each day before work.

WEEKLY HOME ROUTINE

Monday	Pay bills with online banking. Stay home.
Tuesday	Grocery shop.
Wednesday	Shop for needed items or free night.
Thursday	Do errands: banking, post office, and returns.
Friday	Cut grass and clean up house.
Saturday	Yard work, golf, or skiing.
Sunday	Go to church and relax.

Jackie and Bill started to expand their social network once their home and personal chores were under control. They put the spark back into their relationship despite the empty-nest syndrome and looked forward to enjoyable activities on the weekend.

A New Way to Keep Up

Instead of burdening your mind with reminders, such as "I need to sew on a button," or "I wish I had time to pick up a few plants," or "I should have e-mailed the team yesterday," create a dependable schedule on paper or your computer—where you can see it and refer to it. Reviewing to-do lists from the last few weeks may help you see a pattern of general categories that need your attention. Schedule the ones you most often neglect or overlook.

Take a moment now to walk through the following three steps:

STEP 1: IDENTIFY THE REGULAR TASKS YOU ARE NOT FINISHING. Pick one area to focus on for the next two months until you have a comfortable schedule that works.

STEP 2: POST A MONDAY–SUNDAY CHART. Simply draw a chart on an index card and fill in with pencil what you think will work. Keep the pencil and eraser nearby so you can adjust the chart as you live it.

STEP 3: POST THE CHART WHERE YOU'LL BE ABLE TO SEE IT AND ACT ON IT. For example, put your work chart on your computer monitor or on the corner of your desk. Tape your personal chart to your bathroom mirror, and place your home chart by your kitchen sink.

> ## Time-Saving Tip #50
>
> Set up a computer reminder system to help you remember your weekly tasks, such as e-mailing your staff Tuesdays at 9:00 a.m., turning in your expense reports Thursday at 4:00 p.m., and producing your weekly report on Fridays at 1:00 p.m. The more you do this, the more of a natural habit it will become.

It Sounds So Simple

All of this may sound simple. We're trying to free up your time and save you from the crisis that can result when you make too many decisions in a day. This reminds me of the chart I made for my daughter Lisa when she was in kindergarten.

She'd wake up and whine each morning before she even got out of bed, "What's gonna happen today?" Her little short-term memory rebelled without a plan, so I posted an index card by her bedroom light switch that she could read as she went to bed at night:

LISA'S KINDERGARTEN ROUTINE
Monday—Show-and-tell: return folder
Tuesday—Gym
Wednesday—Music Makers, snack supper, Space Cubs
Thursday—Library; Bill Cosby show
Friday—Play with a friend
Saturday—Cartoons *after* 7:00 a.m.

Sure enough, it worked. By having a dependable routine, Lisa looked forward to each day. Her schedule was in order, she had time to prepare for school, and her outlook became more positive.

Adults, too, work more effectively when we preplan routines that keep our lives humming. We have a feeling of security when we know what to expect. You can simplify your time by creating a chart of those chores that now plague you. Then eliminate worry and guilt by completing each chore on the designated day.

Are You Game?

Pull out an index card and jot down what you could improve by doing each task on the same day weekly. What strategic actions could you take now that will help you easily put your week in order?

Practice the actions on your list at the same time each week until they become part of your routine. Once you've established a predictable rhythm, you can toss the chart. Now you have one more way to start living with the extra time savings.

It's Your Time
Create Weekly Time-Saving Routines (Time Tool #7)

☐ Post an index card at work and one at home where you will see them often.

☐ Make note of regular tasks that help you feel on top of things.

☐ Put down one action per day that will keep your life simple and in order.

By initiating certain routines, you can lessen the time and energy expended when it is necessary to make the same decisions day after day. You will be able to schedule your time more efficiently and even combine certain activities.

—Lila Empson

Time-Saving Skills
to Simplify Your Lifestyle

• •

Now that you're on the road to success with time-saving habits and tools, let's add a higher level of time management skills to balance your life despite rigid deadlines and demanding schedules. Stop running and learn how to leverage and multiply time.

WEEK 3
Time-Saving Skills to Simplify Your Lifestyle

Day 16	Take Time for Relationships
Day 17	Simply Find More Personal Time
Day 18	Discover Your Rhythm for Each Week
Day 19	Master the Secrets of Successful Multitasking
Day 20	Overcome When You're Overwhelmed
Day 21	Learn to Delegate and Say No
Day 22	Take Some Downtime Each Day

Take Time for Relationships

My granny taught me, "Be nice to everyone, but pick your friends." And "If you have three good friends in your life, cherish them." The other day I decided to count my true friends through the years. I have thirty! What a blessing.

—Thelma Wells

While visiting my daughter Christy at college for a couple of days, I tagged along to some of her daily activities. As we slid into a booth at a local coffee shop, she explained, "I get paid as part of an internship to sit with a high school student while she does her homework twice a week." She caught the look of concern in my eyes. "Don't worry, Mom. I can study for my classes too."

At that moment, a high school girl showed up. We smiled and greeted her. Christy's teacher walked in a few minutes later and motioned me to her table.

We settled down for a talk, and Mrs. Somerville explained the situation. "You are watching a program we have in cooperation with an alternative high school. Studies have shown that if at-risk high school students have five regular adults in their life each week, they will thrive. We want our student teachers to learn to build relationships, not just information, into the lives of their students."

With that, I learned a valuable lesson: we put ourselves at risk without seeing friends regularly. You can adjust your own quota, but for now strive for five friendly encounters each week.

Where Do I Find Time for People I Care About?

Time-Saving Tip #51

Program your friends' and family's phone numbers into your cell phone or on speed dial on your home phone. When you have a spare moment, surprise them with a call.

Think of the five strongest relationships in your life right now. How many of these people will you see this week? How many will you talk to on the phone? Or do you e-mail to keep in touch?

It might be rare to see all five friends in one week. But to stay connected, there has to be face-to-face time and other ways to stay in contact. My personal motto is, "If you're in my calendar, you're in my life." After all, people in your calendar *are* your life!

How many times has a friend said, "We should get together. I'll give you a call." Or perhaps the person suggests that you call her. Don't agree to that. Instead, schedule a get-together on the spot or assume it's not going to happen. It all comes down to scheduling.

Ten Ways to Make Time for Relationships

1. MAKE CALLS WHILE DOING MUNDANE TASKS. One busy mother calls a friend each night while she washes dishes. A busy teacher calls her elderly parents each morning on her drive to work.

2. LEAVE A REGULAR LUNCH TIME OPEN. A minister was often asked to get together with new people, so he set aside Tuesday and Thursday lunch hours for anyone who approached him at a weekend service requesting an appointment.

3. E-MAIL APPRECIATION. At Thanksgiving, one lady e-mailed me about how much my book *Simplify Your Life* had changed her life. She said, "In taking stock of who to thank this year, I wanted to let you know you were one of the top ten, even if we've never met. Thank you!"

4. SEND "THINKING OF YOU" NOTES. When I was a child, my aunt Helen wrote me a note with a joke or pleasant thought every Monday when she got to work. Perhaps that's why she's one of my favorite aunts.

5. SEND A CHRISTMAS LETTER. Make new friends but keep the old by sending Christmas cards. This is a golden way to hold on to those past and long-distance relationships. Good friends from the past appreciate the yearly check-in.

6. DO SOMETHING TOGETHER. Build a friendship or keep one going by doing something together that you both enjoy. Join a gym, plan a walking schedule, or go to a conference together. It's the quickest way to spend quality time with a new or old friend.

7. JOIN A GROUP. Look for people who share one of your favorite hobbies and make some new friends. When you camp or cook together in a class, you generally attract like-minded people.

> **Time-Saving Tip #52**
>
> If you are short on time to spend with people, here's a solution. Greet three people at every meeting you go to. It only takes a few minutes with each person to keep in touch.

8. VOLUNTEER TO SERVE. Whether you're a person who is usually in charge or one who typically follows, try something new. Jump in and serve as an usher for a sporting event, concert, or play, or plan a luncheon at work. This gives you a chance to make new friends and to find out things about people you already know.

9. VACATION TOGETHER. Organize a spa weekend for women of all ages, or a golf outing, or a couple of days at a resort. A weekend away with friends provides quality time to catch up.

10. DO SOMETHING SOCIAL EACH WEEK. Though it's nice to relax alone, it's also important to connect with other people. Plan a social event with someone else once a week, or call a friend you haven't talked with in a while.

Starting from Scratch

When we moved from Illinois to New York, I didn't know anyone. I had two toddlers at the time and felt very isolated. I wondered how I could make

Time-Saving Tip #53

Look for ways to call,
e-mail, or dine with
friends you want to
have in your life a
year from now. Plan a
pleasant future by
spending time with
them now.

new friends, go out to lunch, or attend an event when I didn't have a babysitter or a relative to help me. My loneliness prompted me to create an action plan.

I thought of the people I would like to have as friends. There were many interesting people, but how could I connect with them since most worked outside the home? I changed my focus. I decided to approach three mothers from my kids' preschool and from our church who had a time schedule similar to mine. I put the three names and phone numbers by my kitchen phone. And I called only one each week so I wouldn't infringe on their time.

Six months later, we had a storm that dropped two feet of snow. After shoveling through the snowdrifts in our driveway to get home, I found three messages on my answering machine, each one expressing concern for our safety. Who were they from? My three new friends—the women I had consciously called over the previous weeks. I had made friends!

Create Win-Wins in Your Relationships

One of the purposes of saving time is to spend it with people you enjoy. Plan now to make new friends, cultivate old friendships, and focus on your family in positive ways that create a win-win for everyone. Soon you'll be surrounded by people who appreciate you and you them.

It's Your Time
Take Time for Relationships (Time Skill #1)

☐ Think about your "strive for five" weekly friends and what you like about them.

☐ Let these friends in your inner circle know how much you appreciate them.

☐ Look for ways to give these five friends meaningful time and attention.

Friends are people you make part of your life
just because you feel like it.

—Frederick Buechner

simplify your time

Day 17

Simply Find More Personal Time

So here is the dilemma: How can we be friendly
toward ourselves without being decadent? Hmm . . .
maybe two long bubble baths a week, not two a day;
two truffles a month, not two an hour; two walks
a week, not couch potato-itis.

—Patsy Clairmont

Deanna and René walked out to the parking lot together. "What are you doing this weekend?" asked Deanna. "We've got Joey's soccer game, Lindsay has a birthday party to go to, I have grocery shopping and cleaning, plus dinner with my parents. I'm tired before it even starts. I wish I had some time for myself."

René responded, "That's interesting. We'll probably see you at the soccer game and the birthday party. Why don't we carpool getting the kids to the party? I scheduled a deep massage and facial at the spa near there. I've been so stressed with work lately that I thought I would treat myself while the kids are at the birthday party."

"Why don't I ever think of something like that?" Deanna responded. "I just don't have the time or money. Maybe someday when the kids are grown and gone."

René laughed. "Why wait until then? You won't last that long if you don't take some time for yourself. Maybe you could call the spa and join me. I'll teach you how to enjoy life."

When Do I Get Some Personal Time?

Life is so busy that often the last item on our to-do list is taking personal time. Why do we always put ourselves on the bottom rung of the priority list and then wonder why we're so tired? If we were well nurtured, we would certainly experience more personal joy and less burnout. But our personal life is often taken up with home and family before we can get around to that narrow niche of time we call personal time.

We've been taught (and often thought) that spending time on ourselves is selfish. Most of us basically live for work, family, and others crossing our paths of life. Enough of that already! It's time to see how personal time benefits all three of those areas and how you can maintain the pace of life you desire.

What Is Personal Time?

Personal time is

- time given to refresh yourself physically, mentally, spiritually, and emotionally;
- time spent in a peaceful and relaxing way; and
- time unrushed in a satisfying personal activity.

Personal time is more than a bubble bath; it's a bubble bath that leaves you refreshed. Personal time is more than reading a book; it's reading that leaves you satisfied and aware that life is good and you're going to be OK. Personal time is more than a leisurely nap on a sunny afternoon; it's waking up feeling rested.

> ### Time-Saving Tip #54
>
> "Sometime" is not a space on the calendar. Personal time has to happen in real time, so schedule an hour each week for something you like to do.

Personal time changes your mood. It refreshes your outlook. And it renews your physical or emotional energy.

Why Do I Need Personal Time?

If you ignore your personal red flags of fatigue, crankiness, and high stress levels, your body and emotions will accumulate the stress and turn it inward. Studies show that stress is the source of many of our illnesses. And the source behind stress is lack of personal care.

You have a choice: pay now or pay later. It costs just a little time each day to take care of yourself but weeks of time to recover later.

Personal Time—the CARE Approach

When you're feeling stressed and overworked, think through the CARE approach. Which kind of personal time do you need? If you learn your own signals, you can be up and running in no time.

PERSONAL TIME—THE CARE APPROACH
Personal *Care*—Take care of personal needs.
Personal *Activity*—Spend time developing a favorite activity.
Personal *Rest*—Relax and rest when you're tired.
Personal *Exit*—Leave work or responsibilities when they're over.

PERSONAL CARE

Personal care includes taking care of your unique needs:

___ Get a haircut.
___ Do your dry cleaning.
___ Sew a button.
___ Schedule a physical or dental appointment.
___ Buy new socks/nylons.
___ Journal your emotions.
___ Floss your teeth more regularly.

simplify your time

PERSONAL ACTIVITY

This is an activity just for you:

___ Make your favorite meal.

___ Play tennis.

___ Go to the gym.

___ Take a hike outdoors.

___ Go for a swim.

___ Have lunch with friends.

___ Go shopping for fun.

PERSONAL REST

Personal rest includes "kicking back" when you need to:

___ Take a nap.

___ Get away for the weekend.

___ Take a personal day from work.

___ Let the kids go away overnight.

___ Bask in the sun and read a novel.

___ Read a magazine and sip coffee.

___ Get a massage.

PERSONAL EXIT

This means stepping away from the stressors of your life from a few minutes to an hour:

___ Leave work early (or on time).

___ Turn off the TV and get to bed earlier.

___ Walk away from a knotty problem.

___ Excuse yourself from a stressful encounter.

___ Leave the office and eat lunch out.

___ Leave your computer and engage in a hobby.

___ Let go of a membership or magazine subscription.

> **Time-Saving Tip #55**
>
> Each day, spend fifteen minutes reading or journaling to renew your time and refresh your inner life. It will multiply your emotional stamina for the entire day.

Do I Deserve It, or Do I Need It?

Personal time is necessary to reduce stress and to live a longer, happier life. You need it, and just for being alive you deserve it! Personal time doesn't have to be expensive, just personally renewing and rewarding.

Time-Saving Tip #56

Like an invitation marked "Personal for Mary Jones," write "Personal Time" on a weekend afternoon or evening at least once a month.

For René, personal time is this weekend at the local spa. For Deanna, a trip to the spa would be another to-do event on her calendar. René would come away feeling refreshed while Deanna would come away stressed. What's the difference?

René wanted something away from home and work after a stressful time. She thought ahead and planned it as a reward, while for Deanna staying home was her idea of relaxing after a stressful schedule. They both need to plan their preference as a part of the rhythm of their lives.

When Do I Find Personal Time?

You have to first decide what you want to do, and then the "when" will follow. Here are some examples:

- Lunch Hours: There are five hours a week to choose from.
- Transition Times: Stop at a gym or shop for yourself on the way home.
- Evenings: Be intentional each night before seven nights slip away each week.
- Saturdays: Putter around the house as "free choice."
- Sundays: Take a Sabbath rest to renew yourself spiritually.
- Moments: Look out the window, breathe deeply, and listen to a favorite song.

How Often Do I Need Personal Time?

If you're living a balanced life, you may not need to take personal time often. You're feeling nurtured, and your personal needs are being met each day. But when you're in a stressful season of life or feel yourself burning out, you need to recognize and attend to your personal care needs. Don't neglect them.

Ask yourself what you like to do and simply find a time slot in your week to do it. When you are renewed and energized, you stop running and really start living!

It's Your Time
Simply Find More Personal Time (Time Skill #2)

☐ List some things on your calendar margin you would love to do during personal time.

☐ What are the three biggest stressors that you'd like to take a break from?

☐ Check off the area in which you most need to take care of yourself:

____ Personal Care: taking care of personal needs

____ Personal Activity: spending time developing a favorite activity

____ Personal Rest: relaxing and resting when you're tired

____ Personal Exit: leaving work or responsibilities when they're over

---

The time to relax is when you don't have time for it.

—Sydney J. Harris

Discover Your Rhythm for Each Week

Even if you're on the right track,
you'll get run over if you just sit there.

—Will Rogers

Once you have your time tools in place, important relationships in order, and favorite personal time activity in mind, you'll be ready to apply one of the best skills I know to simplify your time. I call it "rhythm." It's a weekly ebb and flow that allows you to be at your best.

The secret to creating this rhythm is twofold. First, pay attention to how you currently spend your time. Second, intentionally choose how you wish to spend your time from now on.

Holly's Story: "How Can I Get Anything Done?"

"Hi, Marcia. I'm so glad you're here," Holly said as she opened her front door. Behind Holly stood her husband, holding six-month-old Jacob as two-year-old Joel held on to his mother's leg. They looked like happy but tired parents.

"I'm glad to be here," I said. "And I'm ready to hear your concerns about not getting things done." Theirs was a common complaint—one I often hear from parents of young children. I could relate, but there are time skills to solve that problem.

We moved to the kitchen with a fresh pot of tea, a pad of paper, and a pen. Holly's husband took the boys and headed upstairs. It was Holly's time to get some help.

Start Where You Are Now

"As you can see, the house is picked up—sort of. My husband is helpful, and the boys are really good . . . but I still can't get to some of the things that matter, like laundry and ironing and fun stuff like decorating projects. I feel guilty all the time. What's the matter with me?"

I touched her sagging shoulder and reassured her. "Nothing's wrong. You're just in the busiest time of a mother's life, trying to juggle the constant interruptions of children with your vision of what 'should' be accomplished in a day. I'm here to help you make a plan that works for you."

As Holly disclosed what she did each week, I took notes. Soon she had listed fifteen activities. Then she added another ten that she never got to.

"When you're in a rut like this, Holly, it's time to look at the truth—actually track on paper what you do each hour of the day. Are you willing to do that every day for a week?"

She looked dubious but agreed. I encouraged her, "Just keep the paper in one spot all day, and on the hour, jot down the main action you took. I'll return next week to show you how to use the patterns of time in your time log to your best advantage."

> **Time-Saving Tip #57**
>
> To exercise more, join a gym. Take turns with your spouse. When you have the kids, focus on having fun with them. Plan popcorn and a movie activity to keep them happy.

Tally Your Time in One Week

Each week has 168 hours. That would certainly seem like enough time to keep up with chores and still have a few hours for ourselves. But often it's not, especially if you haven't found or created a workable rhythm for daily living, including meeting the needs of young children.

Here's how to create a time log, like Holly did:

1. Pencil in the 168-Hour Chart for the following three areas:
   - ☐ Sleep
   - ☐ Meals and cleanup
   - ☐ Primary weekly activity (e.g., work, volunteering, parenting, care-giving, etc.)
2. Color these three blocks with three highlighter colors.
3. Total the hours spent on each and write the amount in the margin. Example:
   - ☐ Sleep (49 hours)
   - ☐ Morning routine/meals/cleanup (30 hours)
   - ☐ Primary weekly activity (50 hours)
     Total—129

Subtract 129 hours from 168 hours in your week, and you'll have 39 hours left. Detail the time log in these three categories to discover where the majority of your time is going. You may be surprised.

4. Group the rest of your time in three other categories. Example:
   - ☐ Transition time, such as drive time to work or children's activities (3 hours)
   - ☐ Family/TV/computer time (10 hours)
   - ☐ Meetings or classes (3 hours)

Subtract the 16-hour total from the 39 hours you have left from the first three areas. This leaves 23 hours each week for projects, personal time, relaxation, and fun.

168-HOUR CHART FOR HOLLY

Holly's Goal: Accomplish what I need to and enjoy my week! Boys 2 years + 6 months

	MON	TUES	WED	THUR	FRI	SAT	SUN
4:00							
5:00			SLEEP				
6:00		6—Quiet Time					
7:00			MORNING ROUTINE				
8:00	Wash darks	Grocery	FREE!	Wash whites	Boys' wash		
9:00	& towels	shop		& socks	& towels		
10:00	Project	Las	MOPS	Staff			
11:00	Choice	Madras		meeting			
Noon			LUNCH & CLEANUP				
1:00	Thank	Sweep	Bathrooms		Project		
2:00	yous	& mop			Mentor		
3:00						Family	
4:00		Fitness		Fitness		fun	E-mail
5:00							
6:00			DINNER & CLEANUP				
7:00	Aerobics	Chris		Chris			
8:00	class	to gym		to gym			
9:00							
10:00	10:30–6						
11:00							
Midnight							
1:00							
2:00			SLEEP				
3:00							

1. Sleep = 49 hours   2. Chores = 15 hours   3. Meals = 28 hours
4. Activities = 9 hours   5. Personal = 6 hours   6. Free = ____ hours

Surprise, Surprise!

Typically out of 168 hours, there are ten to twenty hours of "free choice." Holly was discouraged that she could never find that time. But once she saw how to structure her days, she was hopeful that the unstructured hours could be put to better use.

So we added time frames specifically for laundry, cleaning chores, and activities she attended.

Holly looked at her chart. "That looks so much better. I can really see where my time is going. But some of those chores I don't want to do. What then?"

I laughed. "Now that's a whole other session about motivation. You start by thinking of your husband, you, and the children interacting. Picture a happy, well-adjusted family. Then stick to your chart, even if you don't feel like it, because it will make a difference in their lives and in yours. You'll be in control of your time now that you've listed what you have to do and when you'll do it.

Sure, you need to adjust the schedule, but it will work more times than not.

"Use the daytime to handle chores and other routine activities. Then you'll have relaxed afternoons and evenings to enjoy with your children and husband."

Holly looked hopeful and happy. "I'll try it!"

What ideas does this give you for your life? You can simplify your life by taking stock of where your time is really going. Ask yourself if your schedule is bringing you the results you want. Of course, you have to leave several hours open as free time. After you've done that and recognize you are overbooked or underscheduled, you can make changes. You now have the opportunity to balance your days.

Time-Saving Tip #58

To find quiet time for yourself, get up half an hour earlier and enjoy the morning solitude to meditate or read the newspaper and plan your day. This simple action will relieve you of nonproductive hours in the morning trying to get focused.

simplify your time

Your 168-Hour Chart

	MON	TUES	WED	THUR	FRI	SAT	SUN
4:00							
5:00			Example: Sleep (7 hours)				
6:00							
7:00							
8:00							
9:00							
10:00							
11:00							
Noon							
1:00							
2:00							
3:00							
4:00							
5:00							
6:00							
7:00							
8:00							
9:00							
10:00							
11:00							
Midnight							
1:00			Example: Sleep 11:00 p.m.–6:00 a.m.				
2:00							
3:00							

Find Your Personal Rhythm

Intuitively, we do certain things at certain times in the week. We fall into patterns without realizing it. Tracking our actions on paper can jolt us out of time wasters.

If you feel too many things in your life are left undone, copy the blank 168-hour chart and keep track of your time as Holly did. The simple act of writing down the main thing you do each hour will show you how much time you get distracted or spend on time wasters. Then you can create a master plan and reassign those hours to activities that add balance to your life.

Everyone has a weekly rhythm. Those who are most satisfied with life have a balance of personal time, purposeful work, and relational time. Before you fall asleep at night, think about what worked that day and what you want to improve tomorrow. You can improve every day.

Time-Saving Tip #59

Preplan your chores on specific days each week so you only have to think about them once.

It's Your Time
Discover Your Rhythm for Each Week (Time Skill #3)

☐ Track your time for one week on the 168-hour chart. Star two good things you did and two you want to improve.
☐ Find your balance of scheduled and unscheduled time that energizes you each day.

He who would make serious use of his life must always act as though he had a long time to live and must schedule his time as though he were about to die.

—Émile Littré

Day 19

Master the Secrets
of Successful Multitasking

Most people never run far enough on their first
wind to find out if they've got a second. Give your
dreams all you've got and you'll be amazed at the
energy that comes out of you.

—William James

Sheila ran into the house and grabbed the ringing phone. "Oh, Sharon, I'm so glad it's you. I wanted to know when I'm supposed to deliver dinner to Mary and her family. Was it tonight or tomorrow night? . . . Tonight? OK, I think I can pull together a salad, some frozen pot pies, and fresh bread before I need to be there. Have you seen her new baby?"

Sheila continued to listen while she unloaded her groceries and shushed her kids. They followed her into the house and asked for a snack. She put a couple of Pop-Tarts into the toaster and motioned for them to put their things away—all while repeating "Uh-huh" into the phone with Sharon still on the other end. Sheila opened the freezer, pulled out the frozen pot pies, and slid them into the oven.

"Sure, Sharon, dinner tonight is no problem. At 5:30 I have to drop off Jenny at ballet close to Mary's, so it will work. As a matter of fact, I just put the pot pies in the oven, and they will be ready in an hour." Sheila served the kids their Pop Tarts and hung up the phone.

Oh, the joys of multitasking!

What's the Secret of Successful Multitasking?

Some days you group chores together with the ease of an office manager. You're in control, your mind is clear, and every activity falls into place just as you planned. Other days you might feel like a misfit! Nothing works. The faster you go, the less you accomplish. Too many unexpected interruptions can be your undoing. At that point, you may wonder if multitasking is such a good idea.

The secret of multitasking comes down to two words: comfortable momentum. For some people this might mean operating at high speed with six activities going on at once—while doing two things at the same time is a stretch for others. It's all about you and your style. There are ways to determine what is best for you. Let's move from basic to complex multitasking skills.

> **Time-Saving Tip #60**
>
> Start your laundry before breakfast, put it in the dryer after eating, and fold it before you walk out the door. Time saved? An hour of laundry in the evening or on the weekend.

Doing Parallel Tasks to Get Things Done

Simple multitasking begins with two tasks going on at once. Examples:

- Watch TV after dinner and clean the kitchen during commercials.
- Pay bills while your kids do homework at the same table.
- Talk on your cordless phone and dust the living room.
- Water plants while dinner is cooking.
- Jot down menu ideas for the coming week while unloading the dishwasher.

simplify your time

If you time them right, the parallel tasks should be finished at the same time. Usually one is the main focus and the other is a side job that can be completed during the same time frame.

Sequencing Longest to Shortest Tasks

A second kind of multitasking is "sequencing." Start with the longest task first and then place the next logical steps right after it. You probably have been doing some of these already, but use these to jump-start other ideas you can implement.

- Start a meal with the item that needs the longest time to cook, such as lasagna in the oven. Add the stovetop vegetable next and a fresh salad last.
- Start the laundry first thing in the morning. Dry mop the tile or vinyl floors. Dust wood furniture with a feather duster. Switch wash to dryer. Put away paper clutter. Wipe down kitchen and bathroom countertops. Fold clean laundry.
- Drive to the store farthest from home first. On the way back, stop at the shops closer to home.

These scenarios work well for you if you complete the sequence with all the tools put away and the area cleaned up. If you start tasks but don't clean up, you probably are engaging in too much activity. Don't start more than you can complete *and* clean up.

Multitasking the Mundane

A third kind of multitasking passes the time while you accomplish two things at once.

- Put in a load of laundry, and in the half hour it is washing, clean out one or two dresser drawers.
- Iron while watching a favorite TV show.

- Read a magazine or newspaper while walking on the treadmill or riding the stationary bike.
- Set the table for the next meal as you empty the dishwasher.

Multitasking Through Delegation

A fourth kind of multitasking works well when you learn to let go of doing everything yourself. It invites other people in your family to step up to the plate and be responsible.

- Turn over lawn mowing and hedge trimming to your spouse or older child.

Time-Saving Tip #61

Save twenty minutes today by having your spouse or teen pick up milk at the grocery store or dry cleaning on the way home.

- Entrust the care of household pets to one or two responsible children.
- Invite a friend to help you bake holiday cookies.
- Have the kids decorate them while you address Christmas cards.
- Assign one or two rooms to each family member to dust or vacuum every week.
- Delegate family picture development online to one of your teens.
- Pick up the photos on the way home from work the next day.

Work-Related Multitasking

The fifth kind of multitasking helps you keep a balanced life between work and home. For example, you could do any of the following:

- Put a chicken or roast and vegetables in the Crock-Pot in the morning and come home to the aroma of a well-planned dinner.
- Choose a new CD or book on tape to listen to as you drive to work or run errands.

- Gather mail, dry cleaning, prescription refill slips, items to recycle, and papers to copy or fax the night before, and handle them the next day.
- After work, call home to have someone start dinner and/or set the table.

Beware of the Pitfalls of Multitasking

When you overdo multitasking, you cross the line from organized to overwhelmed. Beware! That is much too much, and you should backtrack until you complete each task.

Generally, one to three tasks are all that we are equipped to handle with ease. For example, if you start your morning by washing a load of clothes, reading the paper, preparing breakfast, calling a babysitter, and packing your kids' lunches while signing their permission slips, you are multitasking yourself into a chaotic morning. Something has to give, and usually it's you or your family harmony. Recognize when you've reached your limit. Stop right then and bring closure to several tasks.

> **Time-Saving Tip #62**
>
> Start with two tasks such as sweeping the floor and talking on the phone and enjoy the twenty minutes saved by putting your feet up and reading a favorite book. You earned it!

The Many Benefits of Multitasking

When you multitask appropriately, you regain control of your time by completing the tasks that are a part of your daily life—and add some bonus activities such as listening to CDs as you drive or talking with friends while you wash dishes. You stay up to date by accomplishing your daily goals in a timely way. Instead of wasting time, you multiply it by doing two or more things at once. The reward of multitasking is the time and energy you have for fun and relaxation. You've earned it, and now you have time to enjoy it.

Practice multitasking skills that fit into your lifestyle, priorities, and energy level. Decide what your comfortable momentum is and enjoy the adrenaline flow of doing two things at once. Then reward yourself by doing something you enjoy with the time saved!

It's Your Time
Master the Secrets of Successful Multitasking (Time Skill #4)

- ☐ Note your personal reference point where successful multitasking turns into stress. Avoid it!
- ☐ Write down two or more actions you took simultaneously today.
- ☐ Estimate the time you saved and how you benefited.

Energy and persistence conquer all things.

—Benjamin Franklin

Day 20

Overcome When You're Overwhelmed

Formulate and stamp indelibly on your mind a
mental picture of yourself as succeeding. Hold this
picture tenaciously. Never permit it to fade. Your mind
will seek to develop the picture. . . . Do not build up
obstacles in your imagination.

—Norman Vincent Peale

There are times in life when everything is going well. And then comes the day when you wake up and everything you attempt seems to fall apart. Jan called me after she had one of those days.

"I couldn't believe it. I thought I had a good rhythm in my life, but I had an uneasy feeling I was getting behind. At work, my in-box was higher than normal, my teenagers were a little edgier than usual, and my husband was busy doing his own thing.

"Then Monday I woke up late and didn't have a chance to get anything ready for the day. I had to wash some silverware by hand in order to eat breakfast since I skipped doing dishes for two days. I had to wear a wrinkled blouse since I didn't have time to iron. My daughter woke up sick just when

I was ready to leave. Ugh. I was behind before I started. And I had a report due at work that I meant to finish early.

"I felt so overwhelmed that I wanted to quit my job. It's been a long time coming, but yesterday it really hit. What should I do?"

Untangle Stress

Jan was desperate to get back on track, but there was no letup in her schedule until the weekend, and that was three days away. The mound of to-dos piled up, there was no peace at home, and work wasn't going well either.

A time crisis will often turn into an emotional crisis if you don't stop, breathe deeply, and take stock of what you need to adjust. Let's take a look at some practical steps.

Being overwhelmed also has its benefits. It can bring clarity to your life. Stress can cause you to sit in self-pity or rise up and conquer. It can be an excuse to collapse or a chance to overcome the impending time deadlines. It can cause you to slack off and give up, or change the course of your day with a new plan.

I urge you to welcome the time crunch and consider it an opportunity to crystallize what's really important.

What's Absolutely Necessary?

A time crisis causes you to ask three key questions to move out of the zone of being overwhelmed:

1. What absolutely has to be done?
2. When can I do it?
3. How can I squeeze it in?

Write down the tasks that are troubling you. If you can put them in categories, so much the better. For example, Jan wrote:

Work Crisis:

* Got report in late today.
* Boss isn't happy with me.
* In-box is overflowing.
* Desk and office are a mess.
* Stressed out all day and getting nothing done.

Home Crisis:

* Daughter woke up sick and needs to get to the doctor.
* Dishes and laundry are piled up beyond normal.
* Bills and paperwork are getting out of control.
* The clutter is driving me crazy.

Jan was about to stop there, but I pushed her further. "What about you? How are you feeling about all this?" I asked. "Maybe you're in crisis too."

She responded with a sigh and dropped her head. After she paused, she added to the list.

Personal Crisis:
I can't keep up and I feel overwhelmed!!!

Plan Your Work and Work Your Plan

Jan and I put together a plan. Then I encouraged her not to push herself over the edge. "Make a plan for today," I suggested. "Then get some sleep and regroup early in the morning for tomorrow. Taking it one day at a time means choosing the right priorities each day until you're back on track."

After reviewing her crisis lists, she decided to put her problems in order for that day and add a time frame for each one.

	PRIORITIZE PROBLEMS	TODAY'S ACTION AND TIME FRAME
Biggest Crisis	1. Deadline for work project this morning. 2. Child has fever and feels miserable. 3. I'm personally overwhelmed.	8:30–10:00 a.m. Focus and finish project! 8:00 a.m. Call the doctor for today's appointment. 9:00 p.m. Leave the banquet and go to bed earlier.
Medium Crisis	1. Get to the doctor. 2. Attend banquet tonight and present awards.	11:30–1:00 p.m. covers appointment, child to home, lunch. 2:00 p.m. Call emcee and confirm.
Smaller Crisis	1. Laundry piles everywhere. 2. Dirty dishes all over. 3. No groceries in the house.	Sort wash tonight and get family to help. Catch up with dirty dishes at dinner. Grocery shop after banquet.

Time-Saving Tip #64

Start your day by getting the important things out of the way first to relieve yourself of a long day of stress.

Jan admitted that things had gotten out of control lately, which can happen to anyone. In the crisis moment, her priorities became clear: family first, work second, and herself last. But she was looking forward to dinner out Friday night and sleeping in on Saturday to include some time for herself.

"That's fine as long as you keep noticing when you're skimming and start to accumulate a backlog. That's where problems develop like now," I told her. "I'm sure this is temporary, but let's look at two other ways to prioritize."

Prioritize a Crisis: Time Order or Priority Order

In a crisis time it is important to immediately think clearly or even write down "What is the next action in this crisis?" The two ways to do that are Time Order or Priority Order which keep you from helter-skelter activity.

Time Order walks you successfully from one step to the next to complete a long list. For example, Jan needed to get a doctor's appointment first, write and turn in the important report second. While waiting at the doctor's office, she could call about the banquet. And later she could stop by her office to handle her in-box and e-mail.

Time Order at Work
1. Call doctor.
2. Do report.
3. Call re: banquet.
4. Go through in-box.

Priority Order shows you what to accomplish next but without a time frame. In Jan's case, after work she could shift gears at home and easily follow the Priority Order tasks to pick up groceries, wash the dishes, finish the laundry in progress, and finally sit down with a clear mind to do paperwork. Soon things will be back in order and her daughter well again.

Priority Order at Home
1. Groceries
2. Dishes
3. Laundry
4. Paperwork

Time-Saving Tip #65

Recognize that big deadlines cause stress on your daily life. Delegate chores and prepare for the extra pressure.

Move from Stress to Rest

I talked with Jan a week later. "Once I got my work report finished," she said, "my daughter started to recover, and I got through the big banquet. Everything else fell into place too. The house is gradually getting under control again, and I feel so much better. Prioritizing and tackling the hard things first worked well."

It's Your Time
Overcome When You're Overwhelmed (Time Skill #5)

When I'm overwhelmed, I know I need to do the following:
- ☐ Cut back on my schedule.
- ☐ Ask my family and friends for extra help.
- ☐ Lower my expectations.
- ☐ Other _____

Obstacles cannot crush me.
Every obstacle yields to stern resolve.

—Leonardo da Vinci

Learn to Delegate and Say No

Effective leadership is putting first things first. Effective
management is discipline carrying it out.

—Stephen Covey

By now you have many skills and strategies to draw on to simplify your life and
your time. Yet there comes a point when you realize you must say no. You've
multitasked, you've prioritized, you've planned and replanned, but the reality
is, sometimes you're just out of time.

How I Learned to Say No

I remember the moment I learned to say no. I had been speaking for several
years, with three to four engagements a week. My style was to include two-pocket
folders with handouts for every participant. Our dining room table was the stag-
ing area for my able assistants, my grade school children. One evening at dinner
after a particularly hectic month, the three of them looked at me with solemn eyes.

"Mom, we've decided something," said Lisa. "We're not going to stuff folders anymore."

"We're finished!" echoed Mark.

I was disappointed but not convinced. The next week I invited them to help me. But they refused.

So I had to set some personal boundaries. How many times could I balance family and speaking in a week? Two was comfortable, but three was stressing my family. Right then I made a decision: I would accept only two speeches a week. I then put a check mark on the right margin of my calendar to indicate the week was full.

Three days later, I received a call from a meeting planner asking in the nicest tone of voice, "Marcia, we have received rave reviews about your speaking. Are you available to speak to our group on March 27?"

I'm sure I was blushing with the warm affirmation. I opened my calendar and stared at the check mark at the end of that week. I held my breath and mentally scrambled to figure out if there was a way to squeeze in one more event. But then the faces of my three children popped into my mind and the promise to them and myself. I apologized to the meeting planner and told her I was booked that week.

She wasn't dismayed and asked when I was available. I proposed an alternate date, and she accepted it—just like that.

At that moment I wondered, *Why had it taken me so long to learn this?* All these years I had eagerly given and even sacrificed to fit in the dates requested. And now I found out I could say no and still get hired? I learned my lesson: you don't have to sacrifice yourself to get the results you want. And be wary of flattery, or you may be tempted to give up your personal boundaries and business integrity.

Learn It Once, Apply It Forever

Once you learn what you're giving away when you say yes, it becomes easier to say no. But there are some nuances of saying no that are helpful. You need to weigh the situation and the consequences.

Five Reasons We Say Yes When We Should Say No

Before we talk about when to say no, let's take a look at why we say yes when we shouldn't. Each person is different, but you might say yes because:

1. YOU'RE A PEOPLE PLEASER. It's easier to say yes and suffer some pain working things out to accommodate people rather than listen to their disapproval or disappointment in you.

2. YOU WANT THE BUSINESS. You make work a priority, and you're willing to do almost anything to extend yourself. The word *overextended* never occurs to the person trained never to turn a customer away.

3. YOUR MOTHER TAUGHT YOU TO BE NICE TO EVERYONE. You put the needs of others ahead of yours, regardless of what it takes to fulfill their request. You say yes and then dread fulfilling the request.

4. YOU DIDN'T CHECK YOUR CALENDAR. You only have so much time in your week (168 hours, to be exact). Be sure that when you move something new into the calendar, you take something else out.

5. YOU'VE PARTICIPATED IN A CERTAIN ACTIVITY BEFORE AND ASSUME YOU CAN DO IT AGAIN. Saying yes repeatedly can be a problem if you keep adding events without subtracting any.

> **Time-Saving Tip #67**
>
> Learn to manage your current situation with ease. Your ability to say yes and no improves as you recognize how valuable your time is and where you want to spend it.

What Are Your Red Flags?

For some people, saying no to a request is as hard as saying no to a slice of double fudge chocolate cake when they just started a diet. The first step in learning to say no is to recognize the red flags that signal overcommitment, such as the following:

- Your family complains that you're too busy.
- Your best friend says, "You never have time for me anymore."

- You're the last one at the grocery store before it closes.
- Your eyes are bloodshot from reading e-mails too late at night.
- You work from early morning until late at night with few or no breaks.
- You feel exhausted every day.

Geri's Busy Schedule

Geri overheard me answering questions about choosing a planner to meet your personal and professional needs. She pulled out her planner with some embarrassment. "I have so many things on my calendar, I don't even like to look at it anymore!" I took a peek, and I had to agree.

If your calendar is too full, I encourage you to say no! And say it very loudly to whatever new opportunities entice you to overcommit.

Geri really wanted to add a weekend retreat with her girlfriends to the schedule, but she was a committed soccer mom. "My team needs me. I can't depend on anyone else to set up for the kids' game and snacks."

I jumped in. "Whoa, right there," I said. "No one? If not, then it's time to talk with the other parents."

"I've tried, but people just forget or have excuses. I've sent home schedules with the kids *and* called everyone the night before. It hasn't worked," she complained.

> **Time-Saving Tip #68**
>
> Say no when things are out of control. When things settle down, then you can say yes to some new opportunities.

Delegate to Free Up Time

To delegate successfully, you need to find the best time and method to reach each contact. Some folks still only respond to phone calls, but most read their e-mail. Parents often delegate chores to the family through a chart on the refrigerator. Leaders like Geri can delegate work by e-mail or during meetings. Find out what works for the people you're involved with and then follow up using those avenues.

simplify your time

With some coaxing, Geri decided to go on the retreat and limit her delegation reminders to e-mail two days before. If individuals didn't step up to help, then so be it. She had done her part and couldn't be responsible for others.

Time Is Always a Trade-off

When you say yes to something new, you are saying no to something you already said yes to. Think about that. Time for that new activity must come from somewhere. I've met people who cut back on sleep and eating in order to cram another activity into their lives. When is enough enough? Only you can decide. Examine your schedule. Ask yourself why you keep adding to it.

> **Time-Saving Tip #69**
>
> Do trade TV time for a new activity, but never trade sleep or enjoyable personal time for something stressful or nonproductive.

Choose Your Yeses and Nos and Say Them Clearly

While it is empowering to say no, if you say it too often, people may stop asking you to join them. It's important to know what matters to you. Then you can say an enthusiastic yes when you make a commitment and a clear no when you are unable to. The most dependable people know who they are and are clear about their "yes" and "no."

	I SAY YES TO:	I SAY NO TO:
1.	My spouse and kids	People and events that interfere with family
2.	Saturday mornings at home	Work and trainings that take me away on Saturdays
3.	Ending work on time	Personal perfectionism that keeps me at work longer
4.	My favorite hobby and TV show	Spending the whole evening in front of the TV

Being overwhelmed can be a positive opportunity to get down to the basics of what's really important and rebuild your life from there. All the other offers are easier to say no to or delegate because you now have to make the most of limited emotional energy and available time.

Seek to be as accurate and timely in your commitments as you can. Your goal is to know yourself and your schedule so well that you can give an accurate answer on the spot. Effectively say no and delegate to keep your life on track.

It's Your Time
Learn to Delegate and Say No (Time Skill #6)

The next time I'm asked to do something, I will . . .
- ☐ Say, "Let me check my calendar and get back to you tomorrow."
- ☐ Look for a way to delegate other tasks to free up time to say yes to the request.
- ☐ Answer with a clear no or an enthusiastic yes because I know what's important to me.

If you don't know where you are going, you will probably end up somewhere else.

—Laurence J. Peter

Day 22

Take Some Downtime Each Day

When flying from New York to San Francisco,
we don't allow only three minutes to change planes
in Denver. A much greater margin of error is needed.
But if we make such allowances in our travels, why don't
we do it in our living? Life is a journey, but it is not a
race. Do yourself a favor and slow down.

—Richard Swenson, MD

It was Thursday morning, only four days since I had flown into Colorado Springs to work with an international organization for the week. After training the home staff at noon each day and consulting one-on-one all afternoon, I had made a lot of progress and still had two days to go.

The woman initiating my services was the president's wife, who was a seasoned leader and traveler. In just three mornings, Barb and I had organized everything—her desk and files and stacks of paper from months of travel—and we updated her planner with new pages and skills that would keep her going on the road and at home. She had everything she needed. Or so I thought.

She hesitated as we sat face-to-face in her neat office on the fourth morning. "Can I tell you how I *really* feel?" she asked.

I affirmed her with a nod yet swallowed hard as I prepared for whatever she might say. *What could be on her mind?* I wondered. We had finished everything, and up to this point she had been grateful and enthusiastic.

She took a deep breath and closed her eyes. When she opened them, a tear trickled down her cheek. Her lip quivered. "I'm just so . . . tired."

I reached out to comfort her. It was a tender moment. She let her tears fall. No one knew the stress she felt. This may have been the first time she admitted it to herself or anyone else.

Take Time Out Before You Burn Out

At that moment, I was reminded that getting organized and saying no aren't the only answers to a busy life. It is also crucial to recognize the important part our emotions play in the process of becoming effective and efficient.

> **Time-Saving Tip #70**
>
> Set aside a margin of downtime each day when you can kick back and relax. Pay now or pay later. Now is always less expensive.

I felt as though I were standing at a crossroad in Barb's life. What was the next best step? She needed more than just tips on how to get organized. I took a risk and said, "This is coming from deep within, Barb. Tears often tell the truth about our lives no matter what we tell ourselves and others. Your tears are telling you something. I think you might be close to burnout. Could that be?"

After wiping her tears, she regained her composure and nodded in agreement. "And I'm not sure what to do," she admitted.

Two Choices to Regroup

"You have two choices," I continued. "You can either keep on at the pace you're going, wear yourself down, and take six months to a year off to recover—or you can consciously take time to relax for a few hours or more every day. You need downtime, and you probably haven't had it in your schedule for a long time."

She looked relieved when I presented the second option. "Definitely I need to have some downtime every day. I can't take six months to a year off. There's no way."

"OK, then let's start today." I nudged her from a good intention to the next step.

"Today?" She looked dismayed. "Couldn't we start tomorrow?"

"That's the point," I responded. "You have pushed rest into tomorrow, and now your tomorrows have caught up with you. It's time—today!"

Barb pulled out her planner and scrutinized her sched-ule. "Well, today after we finish I have a luncheon with some leaders I haven't seen in months. Then we have a key staff meeting this afternoon, after which I have to stop by the store to get things before we fly out the day after tomorrow. And then I have dinner with you, and some planning and writing deadlines to do tonight. I guess I will have to . . . give up dinner with *you*!"

I had just lost out on the highlight of my trip, which was to have an inti-mate dinner with Barb. But we both won as she gained downtime and I reflected on the importance of dealing with our inner emotional lives as well as our outward clutter.

Time-Saving Tip #71

Plan ten minutes of downtime after a stressful call or meet-ing before moving to your next task.

What Is Downtime?

Downtime is a pendulum swing from stress to rest. Downtime is getting away from the source of the stress to a place of emotional comfort. Downtime is the way to regroup to restore your focus and perspective. The less you have of it, the more likely you are to burn out.

Our lives need balance, not a task to fill in every minute of the day. We have hearts and emotions that cooperate when we are rested and rebel when we're under stress. After intense work and activities, we need a break. We need time away from routine to counterbalance the stresses of our day.

Readjust Your Life

The next morning Barb reported back that after dinner she sat on the couch staring into space. Her husband came in, lit a fire to cheer her up, and was about to leave to give her time alone to regroup. Instead, she asked him to stay. "We had the best talk we have had in months," she told me. "Thank you for your gift of time that made it possible for us to sit and talk late into the evening. My husband is really supportive and thanks you too." We talked further, and she promised to make changes to balance her busy life.

Barb also organized a support group for five other wives of presidents of nonprofit organizations. They all shared similar challenges, so they made it a priority to attend these monthly meetings when they were in town. Sharing their personal lives in a safe setting strengthened all of them.

> **Time-Saving Tip #72**
>
> Allow twenty minutes of downtime before your next adrenaline-producing activity—a big presentation, an important doctor's appointment, or tax preparation.

Where Can I Possibly Fit In Downtime?

Fitting downtime into your daily schedule is easier than you might guess. Insert a few minutes of downtime during the day doing whatever you like to do to relax physically and mentally, such as the following:

- Enjoy a cup of coffee or tea as a common daily "downtime" experience.
- Watch your favorite TV show (but don't linger to become a couch potato).
- Call your mom or friend to chat after a long day with the kids or at work.
- Use your bread maker to wake up to the aroma of fresh bread each morning.
- Start each day with a walk and chat with a friend.
- Work out routinely to relieve your daily tension.

- Take a nap.
- Smile with only eleven muscles to relax the forty-seven tense ones that were frowning.
- Check your attitude and stress levels on the hour.
- End your day with a good book to unwind.

It's Your Time
Take Some Downtime Each Day (Time Tool #7)

☐ Schedule your favorite downtime activity the next time you feel stressed.

☐ Ask a close friend if he or she thinks you work too much.

☐ Stay connected with friends and share something personal about your life.

Half our life is spent trying to find something to do with the time we have rushed through life trying to save.

—Will Rogers

Time-Saving Strategies to Simplify Your Future

Now in the fourth and final week, you are ready to move to the highest level of thinking and planning—with strategies to help you simply walk into your future. As you look ahead and set realistic goals, your future will unfold more closely to your dreams and desires than you ever thought possible.

WEEK 4
Time-Saving Strategies to Simplify Your Future

Day 23	Jump-Start Your Dreams with a Five-Year Calendar
Day 24	Upgrade Your PQ (Project Quotient)
Day 25	Do Less to Accomplish More
Day 26	Go for Goals That Simplify Your Life
Day 27	Ensure Your Future with a Strong Family Network
Day 28	Stop Time to Handle a Life Crisis
Day 29	Make Today the Best Day of Your Life

Day 30   Start Living—Today!

Jump-Start Your Dreams with a Five-Year Calendar

My interest is in the future, because I'm going
to spend the rest of my life there.

—Charles Kettering

Do you remember your mother (or a schoolteacher) saying you could be anything you want to be if you simply dream it and work hard for it? I don't know about you, but there are still a ballerina and a figure skating champion within me waiting to burst onto the scene. How about you? Perhaps a musician, a teacher, a dentist, a most valuable player, or a rookie of the year?

Life doesn't always result in a dream come true. On the other hand, some of our experiences are better than anything we could have dreamed or imagined. But one thing is certain: you have a future, and it begins tomorrow. What do you want it to be like? Following are some practical step-by-step strategies to help you shape your future and to find satisfaction on the journey.

Time Management Under and Over Thirty Years Old

Time management experts claim that if you are thirty years old or under, you should make three-year plans. If you're over thirty, make five-year plans.

Why? I suspect it's because life changes happen more rapidly when you're in your twenties. After age thirty, past choices tend to dictate your direction and the rate of change slows down.

When I ask my audiences to put together a five-year plan, they are skeptical. But when I ask them how old they are now and how old they'll be in five years, they are astonished. One lady said, "I never thought I'd be that old. I only think of my sister as being that age . . . or my mother!" Suddenly the reality of the passing of time hits.

The reality is that if you don't plan for your future, other people (boss, coworkers, spouse, children) will plan your life for you, or your daily routine will swallow up any chance you have to change your lifestyle. That doesn't have to be true—but too often it is. Don't let it happen to you.

How Can I Possibly Make a Plan for My Future?

If we were to sit down together over coffee, I would give you the following five-year calendar and walk you through the following steps. And by the end, you would begin to see some new possibilities for your life.

simplify your time

JAN. FEB. MAR. APR. MAY JUNE JULY AUG. SEPT. OCT. NOV. DEC.

	Winter	Spring	Summer	Fall	Holidays
2007 (46yr.)	Organize all my paperwork	Pay off all our debt	Lose 10 pounds	Start monthly savings	
2008 (47yr.)	Take kids to Disneyland	Get job for college bills	Free choice exercise	New car	
2009 (48yr.)	Go to the Super Bowl	Son's HS graduation	Free choice exercise	New computer	
2010 (49yr.)	Finish my degree 2 courses	Finish my degree 2 courses Empty storage unit	Free choice exercise	Finish my degree 2 courses	
2011 (50yr.)	Upgrade carpets Finish my degree 2 courses	Triple our savings Finish my degree 2 courses	Free choice exercise	50th birthday in Hawaii	

My "15 Item Wish List" for the Next Five Years:
Be debt free and have a savings.
Take the kids to Disneyland.
Get son through high school
  and off to college.
Finish my degree in two years.
Celebrate 50th birthday in Hawaii.

"More Of" List
More action
More purpose
More family
  memories
More income
More results

"Less Of" List
Less routine
Less maintenance
Less busyness
Less car repairs
Less computer
  problems

simplify your time

Fill in your calendar with this information:

1. In the left margin, write the year and your age for the next five years. This action, more than any other, opens your eyes to why you need to plan ahead. At the end of five years, you'll be five years older whether you make a plan or not.

2. Put a star on key personal dates: Start with your own birthday. Then add significant anniversaries and children's names, ages, and grade levels in September for each year. Include birthdays of parents, children, grandchildren, nieces and nephews, and even your grandparents if they are still alive. This exercise will help you see how quickly time passes and how little time you have with your loved ones. It's a reminder to make the most of it.

3. Fill in any future events, such as a special vacation, date to start graduate school, or job status change. The more information you include, the better.

Think of Fifteen Things You'd Like to Do

Typically, either people have too many things they want to do "someday," or they have no idea what they want to do. I find it's best to hone in on real things that are important to you. For example, make a wish list of things you'd like to see happen in the next five years:

- Take the family to Disneyland.
- Go to the Super Bowl.
- See our children graduate from high school.
- Oldest child and I go to college and graduate together.
- Find a good-paying job for college bills.
- Find an exercise program that is fun.
- Purchase a new computer.
- Buy a new car.
- Triple our savings.

simplify your time

- Empty the storage unit and save money.
- Upgrade the carpets.
- Vacation in Hawaii.

Pencil In Your Wishes for Each Quarter of the Year

Studies show people are willing to do anything for ninety days because it's a reasonable length of time. That's a good way to plan quarterly goals. In our calendar, we're going to place three of our listed desires in each of the next five years, leaving free one of the seasons per year.

By the way, it's best not to plan anything between Thanksgiving and New *— yes* Year's because of the busyness of the holidays.

FIFTEEN THINGS I'D LIKE TO DO IN THE NEXT FIVE YEARS . . .

1.
2.
3.
4.
5.
6.
7.
8.
9.
10.
11.
12.
13.
14.
15.

JAN. FEB. MAR. APR. MAY JUNE JULY AUG. SEPT. OCT. NOV. DEC.

20__ (__yr.)	Winter	Spring	Summer	Fall	Holidays
20__ (__yr.)	Winter	Spring	Summer	Fall	Holidays
20__ (__yr.)	Winter	Spring	Summer	Fall	Holidays
20__ (__yr.)	Winter	Spring	Summer	Fall	Holidays
20__ (__yr.)	Winter	Spring	Summer	Fall	Holidays

* Pencil in your projects and dreams—one per season over five years.

simplify your time

Dreams and Intentions Are Powerful

I remember when I first learned the power of dreams. My husband was asked to teach a class on "life strategies." I sat in the audience supporting him, and in the second session he asked, "What do you picture yourself doing five years from now?"

I thought about our nine-month-old entering kindergarten in five years, and I pictured that in five years, I would probably have a toddler and a new baby. Not that I harbored aspirations to be a mother as my main goal in life, but that did seem like a logical expectation. And sure enough, five years later, we did end up with three children under six years of age. They are now young adults whom we enjoy.

Include "More Of" and "Less Of" Lists

Whenever you reevaluate your time, make two lists: one for things you want "more of" and one for the things you want "less of." Granted, some of the items on these lists will be based on emotions, but include them anyway. Then change the negatives and plan for positives.

When you decide the "what" in life, your mind goes to work on the "how." Be expectant and get ready to walk into your future.

> ### Time-Saving Tip #75
>
> Discuss your personalized five-year calendar with your best friend and/or spouse, and see what they can add. Post it where you can see it often.

It's Your Time
Jump-Start Your Dreams with a Five-Year Calendar (Time Strategy #1)

☐ List your "more of" and "less of" time wishes.

☐ Brainstorm your fifteen-item goal (wish) list.

☐ Print the five-year calendar and add your fifteen goals, one per season.

Reduce your plan to writing. The moment you complete this, you will have definitely given concrete form to the intangible desire.

—Napoleon Hill

Day 24

Upgrade Your PQ (Project Quotient)

Life offers two great gifts—time and the ability to choose how we spend it. Planning is a process of choosing among those many options. If we do not choose to plan, then we choose to have others plan for us.

—Richard I. Winword

"I love everything you're saying about moving ahead in life by making a plan for the future, but I'm stuck right now," began Lynn.

She wanted to finish a guest bathroom remodel and decorating project before hosting a Christmas party for some important people, but time and money were obstacles. Her husband was too busy to do the work himself, and he didn't want to pay a professional to finish. "What can I do?" she asked.

Stuck Between a Rock and a Hard Place

I empathized with Lynn. What could be worse than getting stuck with something that's out of your control? Your contractor quits, your spouse won't help, you run out of money, the materials don't match. Besides doubling the estimated time and money to complete a project, you need to know what to do when you get bogged down in projects.

On the flip side, nothing is more rewarding than to start a project and see it through to completion. As long as time is marching on, why not get in on the action and upgrade your PQ—your project quotient? Your project quotient is your ability to successfully initiate and complete desired tasks that take from three hours to three months. It's one of the most satisfying ways to control your future in a positive way.

What's Your Style?

If you think back to several of your last projects, perhaps you can relate to one of these three trouble spots that can bog you down:

BEGINNING. Slow starters generally hold back for months in making the simple decision to begin. Their motto is, "If it ain't broke, don't fix it!" Remember, staying stable can turn into getting stale. Stretch to make some kind of positive change.

> **Time-Saving Tip #76**
>
> Keep track of your time spent on the project and compare it to your estimated time. After a few projects, you'll be able to estimate with greater accuracy the amount of time needed.

MIDDLE. Fast starters have no trouble starting to repair a broken dishwasher on Saturday morning, but they give up when the hardware store doesn't have the right part in stock. When you're stuck in the middle, always go forward and finish, even if it means driving to a few other stores to find the necessary part. After all, you're already halfway there.

END. Steady starters work through 80 percent of the project but lose interest just before completion when there are only a few remaining details.

You'll feel successful if you bring closure to all projects so you can move freely into the future.

Creating Momentum—Lynn's Story

Lynn's Christmas party came and went without the new guest bathroom. Over the next year, she continued to complain about the unfinished bathroom

simplify your time

and the long list of projects she and her husband had agreed on but never completed. When I saw her recently, she mentioned they were adding a deck to the house and replacing windows.

"Did you ever finish the bathroom?" I asked.

"Yes, and we've done so much else in the last year and a half." Lynn seemed excited to share the process. "We visited a friend's remodeled house and saw exactly what we wanted. Our friend got his crew to finish not only our guest bathroom but our master bathroom too."

Lynn shared that she followed my advice and got three to five estimates thereafter on each project herself. She took a finance course and budgeted their project money. Her CPA husband respected that and became aware of what looked good. *He* actually found the perfect mirror to finish the guest bathroom project.

> **Time-Saving Tip #77**
>
> Leverage a project to coincide with a special event or holiday—but allow an extra 50 percent cushion of time— so you are highly motivated to finish in a timely fashion.

They laugh at the role reversal, and now they work together as a team. So far they have also repaired their roof, put in new flooring, and painted several rooms. They've found their stride and have a list of what is next.

What Kinds of Projects Upgrade My PQ?

There are several categories of projects that upgrade your PQ. Here are a few:

HOME IMPROVEMENT

By doing a home improvement project, you will join the thousands of weekend warriors who know there is a double benefit: first, you get to enjoy the results every day; and second, you reap the financial rewards when you sell your home.

- Paint and redecorate a bedroom each year.
- Replace old carpet.
- Remodel the kitchen cabinets and countertop.
- Upgrade the bathroom lighting fixtures.

ORGANIZING PROJECTS

- Clean up cluttered magazine and newspaper piles.
- Catch up the photo books and display them on a coffee table or bookcase.
- Clear off your desktop and only put back what you like and use.
- Toss old files and relabel the remaining folders.

PERSONAL DEVELOPMENT

- Join a gym or fitness center.
- Get a new hairstyle and clothing makeover.
- Train for a marathon.
- Take advanced courses or complete your degree.

Where Do I Begin?

When considering how to begin on a new project, start with the following:

- The longest time frame project you most desire
- The project that is logical to contractors—roof, then windows, then interior
- Inside project from the ceiling down
- Organizing projects from the visible to invisible storage systems
- Personal projects, beginning with the most gratifying

If in doubt, start with the project that will bring you the most visible and satisfying success. You will enjoy the completed result (and wonder why you didn't do it sooner). It will spur you on to do other projects.

And remember, there are many rewards to completing your projects. Moving out of stability in the "same old, same old" mode of life offers many benefits:

- It keeps you from being bored.
- It gives you a new focus for a season of time.
- It gives you a forward momentum to make your future brighter than the pull of the past.

Become a Person of Action

Julie bought beautiful material for new window valances in her home. She wanted to warm up her family room, but she never got around to making them. When she moved five years later, she regretfully tossed the outdated fabric as well as her dream.

Don't put off till tomorrow what you can start today. Time moves on, and your dream will die if you don't take action. Plan, begin, and complete the projects that will walk you into your future.

Become a person of action. When you can't change your job, your location, or your family, start some personal projects for the satisfaction of making things better. Decide on a time frame, and enlist the help of experienced teachers or friends to ensure you will succeed.

Build your confidence for the future by initiating change and taking charge of the things you can control. Walk into your future with a plan in hand and strategies for completing the projects that matter to you. Finish at least one new project regularly. "Done" brings a positive sense of accomplishment—one you can enjoy often.

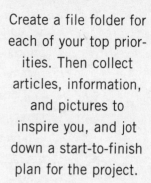

Time-Saving Tip #78

Create a file folder for each of your top priorities. Then collect articles, information, and pictures to inspire you, and jot down a start-to-finish plan for the project.

Time-Saving Tip #79

Once you learn to initiate and complete projects, you have a strategy to control change in your future.

It's Your Time

Upgrade Your PQ (Project Quotient) (Time Strategy #2)

☑ ☐ Set up a file folder with pictures, brochures, and referrals for each project.

☑ ☐ Include no-cost steps such as selling or donating things you no longer need or want.

☑ ☐ Leverage your top three projects with a holiday or special event completion date.

Change is apt to occur when we realize we can change. This is the greatest motivation of all. Nothing sparks the fires of desire more than the sudden realization that you do not have to stay the same.

—John Maxwell

Do Less to Accomplish More

> A high-quality life has a lot more to do with what you
> remove from your life than what you add to it.
>
> —Cheryl Richardson

If you've ever dreamed of finishing your work and walking away stress free, you can. The key strategy is to do less in order to accomplish more. Sound impossible? It's not—once you know where and how to focus your time.

A wise Italian economist named Vilfredo Pareto developed a principle that leverages more accomplishment from less activity. It is called Pareto's Principle or the 80–20 Rule. Here's the premise: 20 percent of your tasks bring in 80 percent of the results. So identify the key 20 percent of your work that brings the desired results to improve your productivity and efficiency. Focusing on the strategic 20 percent will allow you to do less and accomplish more. Let's look at some examples.

Define Your Role, Define Your Focus

Ann had trouble calling new customers even though she was excited about her new job. When she was a stay-at-home mom, she focused on the kids and their school, laundry, meals, and carpooling. But when she became a single mom and opened a home-based business, she had trouble using her time well.

Why? Ann's work had changed, but her setting and self-image hadn't. She needed to change her perception of herself from a stay-at-home mom to a business owner. Her time activities at her home office also needed to change.

I always ask new clients to describe their role and the three main activities that accomplish that role. Next, they estimate what percentage of their time goes there. Then we track their time to see if it really matches. Suddenly they are able to accomplish more in less time because they know where to spend their time.

For example, here are some general ideas:

Entrepreneur—Follow up on new business leads and clients (10%), advertise (10%), build the business (80%)

Corporate leader—Cast vision and manage direct reports (20%), run company and manage meetings (80%)

Small business owner—Fine-tune the systems (10%), train employees (10%), complete the work (80%)

Employee—Report to boss (10%), be a team player (10%), do the job well (80%)

Mother—Homework and carpooling (20%), time with children (40% depending on their ages), meals, laundry, housekeeping (40%)

Student—Attend classes (20%), study (40%), earn income (20%), socialize (20%)

Accomplish More of What?

"Millionaires don't watch TV, or no more than an hour a day," proclaims Dr. Denis Waitley, performance psychologist for Olympic athletes, astronauts, and Fortune 500 executives. So what are they doing less of to accomplish more and still relax? Millionaires avoid mindless TV shows and instead focus on other recreational or social events that promote their personal or professional goals.

How About You?

You may not aspire to be a millionaire, but where you do and do not spend your time speaks volumes. Following are some examples.

John considered whether to advance his career with an MBA degree, which would take two nights of class a week for seven years. At the time, he had two young children, which meant he would be tied up evenings and weekends during their kindergarten through fifth grade years. He decided to do less outside activity to accomplish better parenting. Twenty years later, he says it was the right decision.

Michelle was a single mother who worked days and nights during the holiday season to ensure her daughter a college education. But when her jobs interfered with her time with her high school daughter, she realized what was truly important—being at home with her teen. She quit her part-time positions and asked for a raise at her day job, eventually received it, and six months later earned a promotion as well.

> **Time-Saving Tip #80**
>
> Apply Pareto's Principle each day by focusing your efforts on the important 20 percent of your tasks that yield 80 percent of your productive results.

Twenty Ways to Do Less and Accomplish More

There is only so much time in a day, so let's look at some time savers. What exactly do you want less of and more of?

I wish for less . . .

_____

_____

I want more . . .

_____

_____

> **Time-Saving Tip #81**
>
> Replace your non-productive activities with important tasks, and watch your accomplishments double each day.

DO LESS	ACCOMPLISH MORE
1. Less e-mail time	More projects finished
2. Less TV time	More time on personal hobby
3. Less work hours	More free time in evenings
4. Less clutter around	More beauty and peaceful surroundings
5. Less driving of kids	More carpooling and friendships
6. Less meal prep and cleanup	More shared meal responsibilities
7. Less time for one-on-one socials	More time driving together places
8. Less trivial work	More focus on priority tasks
9. Less distractions	More accomplishment
10. Less Starbucks	More money in pocket
11. Less mail	More requests to remove name
12. Less yard work	More Saturdays relaxing
13. Less bill paying	More online banking
14. Less laundry	More independence for children
15. Less stress	More intentional activity changes
16. Less household pickup	More monitoring the household
17. Less paper piles	More filing and shredding
18. Less responsibilities	More focused choices
19. Less to do	More delegation and elimination
20. Less working late	More completed actions during day

Graphic Artist Changes Her Ways

I met Sherry at a conference where I was speaking. She was really intense—and tired. "It's not fair," she began. "I'm a graphic artist with my own print shop. I start at 7:30 a.m. and I'm still going strong twelve hours later. I can't keep this up much longer. There's nothing I can change except quit the business, yet we need the money."

I asked Sherry how she spends her time each day, and we discovered her pattern. She felt making money was the goal of the business, so she devoted herself to responding to customers' phone calls, drop-ins, and consulting (which she didn't get paid for). Instead of using her expertise by focusing her time on graphics, Sherry spent 80 percent of her time on her least favorite activity—bookkeeping.

Sherry needed to accomplish 80 percent more work for income, so she adjusted her graphic design time to early in the morning, made a plan to find a bookkeeper, and opened the shop at 9:30 a.m. She gave up the busy-work of bookkeeping to accomplish more of her goals related to graphic design. It paid off and she was happier with the time reallocation.

Time-Saving Tip #82

Save an hour of stress at the end of your work-day by accomplishing the task for which you earn the highest dollar early in the morning (or at your most productive time). Guard that time as your most treasured time slot.

Focus on Your "More Of" Items

Before you can focus on your "less of" items, you need to have a mental picture of what you want more of. Is it more relaxation time daily or on the weekends? Is it more projects completed or more face-to-face time with clients or family? More time to put into your hobby?

Here are some people who found more time for a hobby, more savings, more time with family, and more closure at work.

- Jerry wanted more time to restore his sports car, so he did yard work and chores Friday evening. Then he had Saturday free for his hobby.
- Sarah wanted to build her bank account, so she planned meals at home and saved seventy-five dollars a month by not eating out.
- Juanita was tired from working nights at the post office, so she trained her children to make lunches each morning and delegated housecleaning chores.

- Bill had a desk full of customer orders, so he developed forms to simplify the system. He decreased his administrative time by 50 percent by completing them as they came in.

Accomplish More by Reducing Stressful Items

Accomplishing more is a good way to build personal satisfaction into a very busy day. The best way to accomplish more is to get right to the important tasks. Here are some examples of people who wanted to accomplish more by reducing their stress:

- Wendy cut down on chauffeuring her kids to sports and band practice by forming car pools with other parents.
- Josh and his wife, Katie, wanted to divide their mail duties, so she tossed the junk mail and responded to requests while he paid the bills and filed the receipts.
- Joan eliminated stress at home looking for lost homework and keys by hanging a key rack at the back door and assigning the kids a place to hang their backpacks.
- Mike reduced his daily job stress by spending six months outside work to update his résumé, network for a new job, and research available jobs with a goal to advance his career and job satisfaction.

When you do less of what you don't want to do and focus on the main items that produce results, you can go home on time and less stressed. Shift your focus to result-oriented activity, and soon your time wasters will disappear.

Time-Saving Tip #83

Keep a time log for one morning and notice how much time is lost with a slow start, morning interruptions, and attempts to get back on track.

It's Your Time
Do Less to Accomplish More (Time Strategy #3)

To accomplish more in less time . . .
- ☐ Decide which weekly activities are time wasters and which have high benefits.
- ☐ Let go of one time-wasting activity and replace it with something you like.
- ☐ Guard the time when you produce the most by scheduling it as "prime time" each day.

A successful individual typically sets his next goal somewhat but not too much above his last achievement. In this way he steadily raises his level of aspiration.

—Kurt Lewin

Go for Goals That Simplify Your Life

If you're always striving to find some new way to grow, to improve, to better your skills and talents, you'll always be successful, both in the eyes of others and in your own eyes.

—Cynthia Kersey

I chatted with the young gal cutting my hair and watched her attentiveness to her work. "You really do a good job. Have you always wanted to be a hairdresser?" I asked.

"Yes, I enjoy helping people feel better by giving them the right haircut and style," she answered, and we continued to chat.

On a whim I asked, "So what are you working for?"

Michelle stopped cutting and broke into a smile. "A red Mustang. I've always wanted a red Mustang like the ones I see in the movies." And she continued to describe how she was putting aside her money and how much she would need.

When I paid at the counter, I said, "Here's my money, and here's a tip for Michelle."

The receptionist and the other hairdressers turned their attention to me when I handed over a twenty-dollar bill. "Wow, what's that for?" they asked.

"It's for Michelle's dream—her red Mustang." They looked puzzled. Apparently they hadn't heard about Michelle's goal.

"I want a new car," one of the other hairdressers cooed.

Soon the others chimed in, "Yeah, me too."

"Ah," I added, "but Michelle has turned her wish into a goal. She's focused and about to make it a reality."

Goals Are Contagious

Everyone has dreams and desires, but not everyone crosses the imaginary line that moves them into achievement. Goals are the part of life that make us come alive, motivate us to do more than usual, and set us apart from living an ordinary life

Goals are personal, and everyone should have them. They are the quickest way to focus your energy and simplify your time.

What If I Don't Have a Goal?

If we don't include goals as part of managing our time, we only have more of the "same old, same old" routines in life. But if you're like most of us, you want to live your one life fully. Take a minute to make a list (long or short) of the activities, actions, and possessions you'd like to acquire or improve over the next several months or year.

If you want to feel satisfied, happy, and confident in your life, create one or more goals and then take the steps necessary to turn your desires into action. Grow your gifts and talents into their full potential by reaching for the next level. You'll never regret having given it your all.

> ### Time-Saving Tip #84
>
> To see a change a year from now, set your goals for twelve months from today.

Getting Started

A goal is an aim or intention that captures our imagination and compels us to take action until it is accomplished. As Denis Waitley says, "A goal is a dream with a date attached."

Look at your goals as believable and achievable. Then follow these steps as you write down each one to ensure that your goals are SMART—specific, measurable, attainable, realistic, and tangible.

SPECIFIC. Your goal specifies who, what, when, where and why. "I am writing my best-selling book and changing lives."

MEASURABLE. Your goal includes time frames of when and how long. "I will lose ten pounds by my birthday on July 30 this year."

ATTAINABLE. Your goal mobilizes resources and talent so it becomes closer to achievement. "I will learn Japanese by signing up for a course and having a tutor three times a week."

REALISTIC. Your goal represents an intention you see as real with achievable progress. "I will read one book a month to grow my business skills and increase my bottom line."

TANGIBLE. Your goal can be experienced by the five senses—taste, touch, smell, sight, and hearing. "I am sitting by the fireplace enjoying the music and laughter of friends in my decorated family room by Thanksgiving this year."

What's the difference between a wish and a goal? A goal

- has measurable steps;
- begins with an action verb;
- lines up with your interests and values;
- is something you think about often; and
- is in harmony with who you are.

A wish may include several of the points listed above, but it focuses on the distant future (a dreamy "someday") at an undisclosed time without personal action steps attached.

An example of a wish: "I wish I could finish my college degree sometime."

An example of a goal: "Two years from May, I will have my bachelor of arts degree."

Initiate Change by Setting and Achieving Goals

Select a goal by choosing an area in which you'd like to grow. For example, when we moved into a new home that needed fixing up, my husband and I decided to tackle one project every season and be finished in four years. We plodded along room by room, but it was worth the effort because we were very happy with the result.

At the end of our four years, I met a client who complained about the decorating she inherited from the former owners of her house. How long had she lived there? Four years! The same number of years we had lived in ours. Without a plan and goals, nothing had changed for this woman. Even her whining and complaining remained the same.

Don't allow yourself to be victimized by procrastination. Instead, initiate change by setting goals and achieving them. As the saying goes, "Little by little, life's a cinch. Yard by yard, life is hard."

Three Key Areas of Goal Setting

ACCOMPLISHMENTS
- What do I want to achieve?
- What level do I want to attain and improve on?
- What would be one way I could enhance my skills?

RELATIONSHIPS
- Who do I want to spend my time with?
- What kind of people do I want to meet?
- Who are my "strive for five" weekly friends?

ENJOYMENT
- What are the top three places I'd like to travel to and with whom?
- What's my idea of a great vacation and how long?
- What do I want to do in life that I haven't done?

Make One Big "Stretch" Goal

If you tend to think of safe and methodical goals, challenge yourself to make one big "stretch" goal to something beyond your normal capabilities. Your stretch goal could be something that's physically or mentally challenging, such as training for a marathon, beginning a new sport, or entering a competition to advance several ranks. Experience the thrill of trying something new and perhaps even a little crazy. Normal life will never be the same once you've stretched into a new zone each year.

For example, my friend Karen went on her first backpacking trip in the wilderness the year she turned fifty. By the end of the decade, she had hiked to the top of Yosemite Falls, Half Dome, and Mount Whitney. Each year she stretched herself a bit further to achieve the goals she had dreamed about since she was a little girl.

Time-Saving Tip #86

Keep a personal file of yearly goals and accomplishments to ensure you will be a growing, goal-achieving, and interesting person.

When You're Stuck

When you can't think of a thing to change, look at what you achieved last year. Then pick some new goals for this year in the same categories. Reflecting on the status of your life last year is sure to help you move into a satisfying future.

PERSONAL LIFE EVALUATION

My Life	Last Year	This Year
Work	Worked 8:00–5:00 p.m.	Same job, but promoted.
Social Groups	Neighborhood Bunco, PTA, Band Boosters.	Drop Bunco and join an orchestra. Keep PTA and Band Boosters.

Topic	Last Year	This Year
Family Relation-ships and Milestones	Married nineteen years with three kids in junior high and high school.	Celebrate twentieth anniversary in Caribbean. First child to college.
Organizing Projects	Organized my closet.	Organize home office.
Home Improvement	Cut the grass/shoveled snow.	Repair or replace the roof. Get siding quotes.
Physical Fitness	Walked occasionally.	Join a gym.
Spiritual Growth	Attended church.	Join a Bible study.
Income	Earned $60,000.	Add graphics side business.
Savings	Saved 10% net.	Save 15% net.
Satisfaction Level	Everything's OK.	Hire a personal coach to stretch and grow.

Best-Case, Worst-Case Scenario

If you write down your goals, take a moment to read them daily. The worst that can happen is that you miss the time frame you set. No problem. It might have taken a bit longer than you thought, but at least you accomplished them. Or perhaps you'll decide to change one of your goals. Good for you! You're honing in on something more important.

But best-case scenario, you'll accomplish your goal, experience the discipline of perseverance, work through the hurdles and obstacles inherent in the journey, and come out a better person on the other side.

One success inspires the next. Achieve a goal, and enjoy the thrill of focusing your energies and growing as a

> **Time-Saving Tip #87**
>
> List your goals on an index card and place it on your desk or on your bathroom mirror to read every morning and night.

person. Enrich your life one goal, one season, and one year at a time. Then you are more likely to live a fulfilled life.

It's Your Time
Go for Goals That Simplify Your Life (Strategy #4)

☐ Write down three important goals to read every morning and evening for the next ninety days.

☐ State your goals in the present tense as if they are already accomplished. (Example: "I am a successful English teacher and my students love my subject.")

☐ Picture how it will feel to accomplish each goal—where you are, who is with you, what you are feeling—and watch to see what happens!

You control your future, your destiny. What you think about comes about. By recording your dreams and goals on paper, you set in motion the process of becoming the person you most want to be.

—Mark Victor Hansen

Day 27

Ensure Your Future with a Strong Family Network

Do you set aside time to be with your children, partner, sisters, brothers, parents, and extended family? In today's busy world, it's easy for families to drift apart. But you can cultivate togetherness by making an extra effort to "be there" for your children and for other family members— not just on birthdays and holidays, but every day.

—Donna Smalin

As you strategize about your future, you need to think in terms of not only goals, dreams, and aspirations but who will be there with you. Life is fragile, and all the relationships you enjoy today may not be there in the future.

But there is one group of people that will be linked to your past and your present—your family. Your family network may be strong or it may be weak, but there can be mutual benefit if you take the time to stay connected.

Intentional Planning Can Grow into Mutual Friendship

"Mom, you'll never guess who I saw at the conference!" my daughter Lisa exclaimed as she walked in the front door after assisting at a large event. "I was sitting outside the meeting room when I heard someone say, 'Lisa Ramsland, what are you doing here?' And you'll never guess who it was."

By then I was very curious.

"It was my high school girlfriend Erika, who now lives in Oregon! She, her sister, her mom, and her grandmother were on a family 'girls' retreat,' pampering themselves for Mother's Day weekend. Every year around the same time, they meet at a resort. They get manicures and pedicures, shop, and eat out together. Isn't that a great idea? Why don't we do something like that?"

Why Don't We Do That?

FAMILY REUNION

That was a good question. When I got married, I was impressed that my husband's family had weeklong reunions every four years where more than sixty relatives gathered together. And when I was growing up, twenty of my family members got together for a big cookout at my parents' home on Lake Geneva for Mother's Day, Father's Day, and birthdays.

But why didn't three generations of women get together to do "girlfriend" things? I suspected the answer had two parts. First was the lack of time in our busy personal schedules. And second, perhaps we had missed opportunities to be "present" with one another when we were together.

Marry and Bury—There You Are Again

Extended families generally see each other at weddings and funerals. At such times, people connect in a heartwarming way and trade funny stories and memories.

"Do you remember when Uncle Joe tied tin cans on your getaway car and the police stopped you on your wedding night?"

"How about the time we went down to the lake, I caught my prizewining fish, and it jumped out of the boat in the downpour before we got home?"

"Remember the day you got your first bike and crashed into the neighbor's new fence?"

We often think of ourselves in a good light, but relatives have a way of bringing us back to reality! That's when you realize you have come home to people who know you and your past. It can be a special experience. And by the time you say good-bye, you may be thinking, *We should get together more often.*

Build Extended Family Ties

Getting together with extended family can boost your self-esteem by helping you remember who you are and strengthen your family roots. You may come away with a gentler view of life that balances the cares and demands of today. Your family network can be an emotional support that warms your heart with good memories. The happier you are in your personal life, the easier it is to simplify and manage your time.

If you and your relatives live in the same geographic area, make the most of it now, as it may not always be that way. Following are some ways to enjoy family time.

1. HOST NO-PRESSURE FAMILY DINNER NIGHTS. Even if it's only on vacation or holidays, invite relatives over for a nice meal and fellowship.

2. CELEBRATE WITH HOLIDAY POTLUCKS. Make it easy to get together by letting everyone bring a dish.

3. SHARE FAMILY PHOTOS AS A CONVERSATION STARTER. Pictures say a thousand words and help the less talkative find something they can speak up about.

4. TELL A FUNNY FAMILY STORY. Shared memories keep the family history alive and tie the past to the present.

> **Time-Saving Tip #88**
>
> To maintain ties with extended family, make a simple plan to keep in touch by calling on the weekends, e-mailing at the end of the month, or starting a family blog for birthday wishes or other yearly events.

Build Stronger Ties at Home Today

Creating warm relationships for the future begins today at home. We're more rushed than we'd like to be, so we have to be intentional. But there are simple ways to connect with people in your own household on a daily basis. Note these important times and begin to capitalize on them:

1. FOCUS ON YOUR HELLO AND GOOD-BYE TIME. If you had only fifteen minutes a day to allot to your family, spend it with each member when he or she walks in the door. Drop everything to greet your spouse, roommate, or kids with good eye contact and "Hi, I'm glad to see you!"

2. ELIMINATE ARGUMENTS BEFORE MEALTIME. Studies show that most bickering occurs the half hour before people sit down to eat. Avoid this by eating on time and initiating upbeat conversation around the table.

3. EAT TOGETHER REGULARLY. A White House study in 2000 asked what was different in families that had teenagers who "turned out right" versus those involved in drugs, sex, alcohol, and suicide. The answer? Emotionally healthy families ate at least five meals a week together. Even if all five meals are on the weekend, keep mealtime communication open and interesting.

4. TURN OFF YOUR OUTSIDE WORLD AND BE PUNCTUAL. When your son or daughter is in a play or athletic event, put your work aside and be in the front row on time. Children need your presence and your applause. Show up and display your pride in your kids, your spouse, or your roommate. Don't let them down. Be there.

5. RELAX TOGETHER. Sit with your family when they watch TV or nearby while they are on the computer. These two activities can either isolate or bring people together. Change the computer hookups to be in the same room for more together time. Buy headphones if the music scene sends you apart.

> **Time-Saving Tip #89**
>
> Spend thirty minutes over a meal on Friday night to share the highs and lows of your week and save fifteen minutes (or fifteen years) of slowly drifting apart under the same roof.

simplify your time

Time Tips for Families

If you still have children at home, you are extra busy. Here are some key time strategies to apply to family living:

TODDLERS. Be five minutes ahead of them. You can push or you can pull toddlers, but the best way is to lead by always being ahead of them.

SCHOOL-AGE CHILDREN. Be one hour ahead of them. Remind them of what is next—whether school, music, or sports—so they can start to transition mentally and collect what is needed.

TEENAGERS. Be one day ahead of them. If your teenager wants the car on the weekend, leverage his motivation by requiring that he clean his room and do chores beforehand.

SPOUSE. Be three months ahead. If you want to get the house painted in the summer, start selecting colors in the spring. Discuss what you want to accomplish and when you can best do it.

> **Time-Saving Tip #90**
>
> Set a regular time for phone calls to parents or grown children, such as Saturday or Sundays when the weekend rates are low.

Building a Strong Foundation

So much of our time is spent building our careers that we occasionally ← let family time slip. Yet who do you want to be there to celebrate when you earn your retirement gold watch? Or who will support you when you face a disappointing loss or the death of a good friend? Who can you reminisce with about your childhood and teenage years? It's usually the extended family network.

It's never too late to connect with your family. It's one part of our lives we need to make time for. Keep your family networks glowing with the fuel of love and regular connection. When we're happiest, we manage time better and life is simpler.

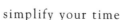

It's Your Time
Ensure Your Future with a Strong Family Network (Time Strategy #5)

☐ What activities other than holiday get-togethers could you do together (e.g., vacation, sports, movies, etc.)?

☐ Who are your favorite relatives, and how can you keep in touch?

☐ Start an online photo gallery or blog to keep in touch despite your limited time.

Placing your relationships at the top of your daily list of activities and spending time to nurture those relationships can help you simplify your life by helping you stay focused on what is truly important—people. Determine each day to keep your relationships in the forefront of your life.

—Lila Empson

Stop Time to Handle a Life Crisis

Only in testing do people discover the nature and
depth of their character. People can say anything they
want about their values, but when the pressure is on,
they discover what their values really are.

—John Maxwell

The man next to me in the airport started chatting after we were informed of
a long wait for our plane. To pass the time, we discussed why we were traveling that day.

When we finished, the airport was filled with commotion as a woman
rushed down the hallway pushing a stroller, her husband grasping the toddler
as she yelled, "We've got to get on that plane—now!" The door to the jetway
was closed and the attendant said no in a firm voice, but the woman caused a
scene by pounding on the door.

My new friend and I looked at each other with a sigh and a smile. He had
shared that he was returning to Chicago from Remuda Ranch in Arizona,
where his teenage daughter was being treated for anorexia. And I had shared
with him the traumatic story of our teenage daughter's health crisis.

As the irate mother finished pounding the airplane door, my seat companion said, "She doesn't know yet that missing a plane is not a big deal, relatively speaking. There are larger life issues, and it's important not to sweat the small stuff."

As my seat companion reminded us both, the irate mother had apparently lost sight of what is really important. Missing a plane is relatively small in the grand scheme of crisis events.

Give Yourself Permission to Stop

It's an important time strategy to know that in a life crisis—whether emotional, relational, or physical—your time will change. And if it's a traumatic incident, then you may even have to stop your normal life for a season.

Give yourself permission to take a life detour and deal with the crisis. Your life may change completely, or it may get back on track in time. Either way, it's all a part of your journey into your future. Let me share three true stories to prepare you.

Lisa's Story—Stopping Time for Our Daughter

When our middle child, Lisa, was a junior in high school, a spinal tap collapsed her health. Overnight, all of our lives changed. What should have been a medical procedure to help her became the beginning of pain and suffering for our beautiful seventeen-year-old. I became a mom with a mission to find help and healing for our daughter.

Each day felt like a week. Each week felt like a month. Lisa's cries of "Mom, can't you do something for the pain?" tore at my heart and sent me to my knees in prayer, desperate for an answer to the prolonged mono, migraines, and fibromyalgia, a lifelong chronic pain condition. Finally, the answer came after eight long months in bed in her darkened room: we found a doctor and a supplement program that started to revive and heal her. Eventually she became active again and graduated from high school and college. Now after eight years pursuing a healthy lifestyle, she is living a relatively full and satisfying life. But it wasn't always easy for our family.

Crisis Time Lessons 101—Focus on the Goal

During our crisis, I focused on two things: getting Lisa well and getting meals on the table. That was it. And it was hard.

As conflicts with time escalated with the change, I asked myself, *What difference would it make if I organized the whole world and couldn't get my daughter through high school or back to life?* Suddenly life wasn't about me, and I took a leave from organizing and speaking to become a full-time caregiver. Crisis quickly refocuses our priorities, however ill equipped we may feel.

You may have to handle more than one challenge simultaneously. My father-in-law suffered from Alzheimer's and then passed away. The same day, my loyal supporter and close friend, Aunt Lor, fell and had a stroke. She died six weeks later. I was devastated.

> **Time-Saving Tip #91**
>
> When a crisis hits, reprioritize your life and give the crisis the time and attention it needs. Regret is a heavy weight, so do everything you can while you have the chance.

Life is not fair, and life can be overwhelming. But do you know what? There's only one way out of a crisis—moving forward. Don't try to stop or wish you could go back. Put your energies into surviving, and at the right time you will move ahead. For us, Lisa bravely finished high school and college. The crisis served its purpose, and I do believe she can now face most anything.

Deb's Story—"This Is Really Bad Timing"

My friend Deb Christensen found out last summer on speakerphone with her husband, young adult children, and physician that she had breast cancer. Her initial response to the news was, "This is really bad timing."

Her youngest child, Jessica, was to leave the next day for her first year of college. Her two oldest sons had just moved home from college and were getting ready to start their careers and get married the next summer. The other son was in college. The anticipated empty nest had suddenly fallen apart.

Deb shared her story. "Immediately I was thrust into the world of doctor appointments consisting of mammograms, ultrasounds, surgeon consultations, MRIs, bone scans, chest X-rays, blood workups, biopsies, and decisions concerning treatment.

"It wasn't until five days later while shopping at the grocery store that the dam burst. All of a sudden I began to cry and wonder how this was going to affect my life and my family's life. Fear set in. Because of my faith, I gave it to God and thanked Him for the great medical team He had given me. I thanked Him for my family's love and support and for the timing of this. There was a reason, I was sure."

Crisis Time Lessons—Take Care of Yourself

Deb continued, "What suddenly became important was first taking care of myself. My husband gave me a leave of absence working for him to focus on whatever I needed—not only for my physical well-being but for my emotional, spiritual, and mental health as well.

"It truly is a pruning process. I began to evaluate what relationships and activities were important to me and what relationships I had to say no to. I focused the three months during my chemotherapy on reading mostly inspirational books, watching movies with deep and uplifting meaning, and laughing at the funny e-mails and books people sent me.

"It became important for me to look forward to the future. I kept picturing my husband performing our sons' wedding ceremonies, and then he and I dancing at their receptions. It's good and important to have something to look forward to like this.

"It seems with cancer it's all about time: chemotherapy for three months, radiation treatments for seven weeks, doctor appointments every three months, and my hair growing back in six months. I find myself measuring my life by the time specifications of my cancer. It has become my new 'normal.'

"Being told you have cancer changes you. It changes how you feel, how you now perceive each day, and how you really want to live your life. I want to spend my time with people who are contagiously positive, lighthearted, and fun, not those who are angry, bitter, or resentful. I have a whole new circle of friends as a result. I've learned to be patient with time. It's also given me a new zeal for life and an appreciation for each day I wake up."

At this writing, Deb's prognosis for recovery is good and she is feeling optimistic.

Martina's Story—"Time Came to an Abrupt Stop"

Martina's life stopped with a shout from the family room. Her contractor husband, Larry, had been on the roof covering a skylight opening with one of their teenage sons when he fell through the roof and suffered fatal head injuries. Her life instantly changed, and so did the lives of her four children, ages ten to sixteen.

She says, "Time came to an abrupt stop for our family. From that moment on we went ahead externally with the memorial service, the funeral, and arrangements. But internally I was numb, and my life was at a standstill. I had been an organized person, but everything about me turned 180 degrees. Family and friends stepped in to carry us through. Immediately I had an entire business to take care of and sell. I spent long hours at it, while my children went from homeschooling to a classroom setting.

> **Time-Saving Tip #92**
>
> Accept that a life crisis is never good timing, but turn it into good by adjusting to your new "normal." You'll find you're stronger than you think.

"Our church stepped in and finished the roof and the flooring project Larry was working on. His dream was to own a cabin in Big Bear, and I fulfilled his dream by working every weekend for four months to complete the cabin he had begun to renovate. We spent Christmas there and talked freely of Larry."

At forty-five, Martina is now a widow, a businesswoman, and a single parent, no longer a homeschooling mom or a wife.

This Is Not for Today

"Time is not the same," says Martina. "I learned when overwhelmed to ask myself if I had to know the answer to the next question in the next fifteen minutes. If I didn't, then I learned to say, 'This is not for today.' It was my initial way of coping. I wrote a lot down to try to remember conversations. A few months later, I was able to think of life for the next half hour. And six months later, I can take half a day at a time.

"I still think and plan for the future, but life is different. You look in the cupboard of your life and experience, and there is not just an empty cupboard; the entire cupboard is missing!"

Martina is one of the strongest women I know. She and Larry were family friends and clients. Now the business of life has been turned over to Martina and the children. She says, "Slowly we grow to a new family unit; shock and emotional stress are still high. But we reach out to each other and receive the practical help offered by family and the eight hundred friends attending Larry's funeral."

Martina was in my summer "Simplify Your Life" class when the tragedy struck. Every time I explained an organizing step, I taught the class to recognize the next steps and confidently say, "I can do that!" Martina applied this when she took over the family business and completed the cabin. However, she worries now about getting her desk and paperwork cleaned up at home. Should she? Not after what she's been able to conquer. One step leads to another as you climb out of crisis.

What Should I Do in a Life Crisis?

"Looking back," Deb concludes, "the timing of my cancer diagnosis allowed me to do more soul-searching than I have ever done before. It was a time of rest. It was a time of cleansing, purifying, and beautification of my inner self. And there's never a bad time for that! Embrace the hard times as much as the good times. God is with you in both."

It's Your Time

Stop Time to Handle a Life Crisis (Time Strategy #6)

☐ Recall your most traumatic event in life and how you came through it.

☐ If you are not in a life crisis right now, look for ways to help someone who is in one.

☐ Thankfully celebrate the joy of living today. This is the time of your life.

Fear comes from feeling out of control. Hope comes from knowing who is in control. And hope comes from knowing that we have a sovereign, loving God who is in control of every event of our lives.

—Lisa Beamer

Make Today the Best Day of Your Life

The people who get on in this world are the people who
get up and look for the circumstances they want, and,
if they can't find them, make them.

—George Bernard Shaw

Today has the potential to be the best day of your life! You could win the lottery or get a call to be on *Oprah*. Today could be the day you finish a long-term project, purchase the perfect outfit, or find your missing refund check. Or better yet, you could find the best rhythm and flow for your day and your week.

There is the potential that today could be the five-star day you've been planning for. It can be a fantastic day, because all "best" days are a date on the calendar. Everything happens in real time. Why not arrange your time so today has the potential to unfold as one of your best days?

When we think of someone's "best" day, we think of a glowing bride lifting her goblet in a toast or an Emmy award winner exclaiming, "This is the best day of my life!" But you don't have to have a milestone moment to proclaim today as the best day of your life. Because today *is* the best day of your life—it's the only day you have. So make it a fabulous day.

How Can I Get Out of the Rut of Normal Days?

There are two steps to begin making today the best day of your life. Step one is to plan in reverse. In other words, begin with the end in mind. Even though it might be first thing in the morning right now, picture yourself laying your head on your pillow tonight and thinking about the great things that happened today. It was terrific—why? Because you did what you planned and you had good things happen along the way. You simply enjoyed how you spent your time today.

Step two is to be open to the uniqueness of the events of the day. Remember how you need to establish the rhythm of your day and week? When we're stressed, it's usually when things are out of control. Don't give up at that point. Regroup and get back on track, even if you don't accomplish everything. Keep the goals for the morning and the afternoon in your radar and keep at them until they're finished.

> **Time-Saving Tip #94**
>
> Make today your best day by planning the day in reverse. Focus on finishing the day with a good feeling and what happened to get that result.

Why Does Today Feel Out of Control?

The three days we have the most control over are today, tomorrow, and the day after. That's because they are closest to the present moment and we can still affect them. But do you know which one of those three feels most out of control? *Today.* That's because the next two days look good in our minds, but we haven't started living them.

To have the best day possible, I believe there are five things you need to deal with every day. As you become a better time manager with each of them, your "todays" will turn out better and better. Here they are in an easy-to-remember acrostic. It's important that you understand each one:

> My Best Day Is . . . TODAY
> I deal successfully with
> T—Time
> O—Obstacles
> D—Destiny
> A—Attitude
> Y—Yourself

TIME. To have a good day, you need to have a regularly good rhythm. That comes with daily using your calendar, a to-do list, and seasonal goals and plans.

OBSTACLES. Overcoming obstacles each day is a feat in itself. Think ahead and allow a cushion of time for interruptions, travel to unfamiliar places, and last-minute details.

DESTINY. You are uniquely created to fill a role and to make a difference in life. Work to succeed at your roles and goals, especially in your circles of influence.

ATTITUDE. A good attitude opens the door to success, so stay positive. Left-brain thinking engages your head, while right-brain responses engage your heart. Use both at the right time.

YOURSELF. Treat yourself well and resist the tangents you create that take you away from your focus for the day. The hardest person to say no to may in fact be yourself!

Time-Saving Tip #95

Focus your attention on the best day this week: today. Use the acronym TODAY to successfully deal with the five elements in a day: Time, Obstacles, Destiny, Attitude, Yourself.

How Skilled Are You Now? A Time Quiz

An important part of capturing the most in each day is to review your time talents and skills. They should be getting better each year as your responsibilities and networks of people increase.

Take a few minutes to see what you apply already from our thirty-day journey. Note where you still want to grow and improve.

Scoring: This is an open-book test, and you may go back to review the chapter before you rate yourself. Score yourself between 0 and 10 (10 being a strong yes) in this area. Now that you've read everything, you can "score" up to 300 total points!

Time-Saving Tip #96

Untangle feelings of stress by using the time tools you needto over- come time wasters.

A FINAL TIME QUIZ

Chapter Topic	Quiz	Score
1. Today *Is* the Time of Your Life	Do you know exactly what you would do with more free time?	
7 TIME-SAVING HABITS		
2. Punch Up Your Punctuality	Do you arrive early at appointments?	
3. Save Time with Two-Minute Pickups	Do you pick up as you go and cut put-away time in half?	
4. Get Off Your Computer and On with Your Life	Do you get off the computer at a reasonable time?	
5. Power Through Your Paperwork	Are your paperwork systems in order?	
6. Clean Up the Clutter	Are your surroundings clutter free and clean?	
7. Plan Tomorrow the Night Before	Have you mastered planning tomorrow the night before?	
8. Change a Habit, Change Your Life	Do you regularly change bad habits for better ones?	

Chapter Topic	Quiz	Score
7 TIME-SAVING TOOLS		
9. Capture More Time with Your Calendar	Do you have three monthly goals on your calendar?	
10. Fine-Tune Your To-Do List	Are you getting accurate with your to-do list expectations?	
11. Pursue a Personal Project List	Do you have a project list planned by seasons?	
12. Put It All Together in a Planner	Do you have a planner for your calendar, to-do list, and project list?	
13. Practice the Power of Prioritizing	Do you prioritize your tasks and stick to them?	
14. Spruce Up Your Support Tools	Are the tools you use every day organized?	
15. Create Weekly Time-Saving Routines	Are your daily routines keeping things in order?	
7 TIME-SAVING SKILLS		
16. Take Time for Relationships	Do you "strive for five" friends you contact each week?	
17. Simply Find More Personal Time	Do you enjoy personal time regularly?	
18. Discover Your Rhythm for Each Week	Are you happy with your weekly routine?	
19. Master the Secrets of Successful Multitasking	Do you multitask and still complete things?	
20. Overcome When You're Overwhelmed	Can you overcome when you're overwhelmed?	

simplify your time

Chapter Topic	Quiz	Score
21. Learn to Delegate and Say No	Do you confidently say yes and no to opportunities presented?	
22. Take Some Downtime Each Day	Do you avoid burnout by taking downtime regularly?	
7 TIME-SAVING STRATEGIES		
23. Jump-Start Your Dreams with a Five-Year Calendar	Do you have a five-year plan based on age milestones?	
24. Upgrade Your PQ (Project Quotient)	Do you control change by completing projects?	
25. Do Less to Accomplish More	Are you doing less and accomplishing more?	
26. Go for Goals that Simplify Your Life	Do you have goals that unfold your future?	
27. Ensure Your Future with a Strong Family Network	Have you grown through a life crisis?	
28. Stop Time to Handle a Life Crisis	Do you have regular contact with family?	
29. Make Today the Best Day of Your Life	Do you enjoy today as the best of all your days?	
30. Start Living—Today!	Are you ready to start living your purpose and dreams today?	
	TOTAL SCORE	

Congratulations! You have improved your ability to simplify your time just by carefully taking this quiz and reviewing the entire book. You will never look at your watch or calendar without asking, "What do I need and want to do right now?"

Make Today Your Best Day

Time-Saving Tip #97

Keep your words positive about your day, and your attitude and actions will follow.

Make today the best day of your life. Why? Because there is only one day you can control the outcome of. And that's today. As coach Lou Holtz says, "Every day, some ordinary person does something outstanding. Today, it's your turn!"

It's Your Time
Make Today the Best Day of Your Life (Time Strategy #7)

- ☐ Don't procrastinate on something you are going to do anyway.
- ☐ Do all your to-dos today. There will be new ones tomorrow.
- ☐ Delete or delegate tasks that keep you from enjoying today. Live one day at a time.

Go confidently in the direction of your dreams.
Live the life you have imagined.

—Henry David Thoreau

Day 30

Start Living—Today!

An average person with average talent, ambition, and education can outstrip the most brilliant genius in our society, if that person has clear, focused goals.

—Brian Tracey

This is it! We're on the last day of our "time" journey. You've learned how time-saving habits add more hours to your life and how to subtract activities that waste time. You also know the value of arriving at events on time, how to multiply the hours you have by doing several tasks at once, and how to divide time into segments in order to fit in more pleasurable activities.

You've learned how to boost your well-being with good relationships, which always simplifies time. All of this is rooted in a good, sound time management system—your daily and monthly calendar, your planner, and a to-do list for every day.

You've discovered how to tighten up your habits in order to limit the time you spend on routines. You know the importance of getting off your computer and on with your life, how to power through daily paperwork, and how to clean up the clutter that's bogging you down.

Now that you have so much going for you, it's time to solidify what you want to do with your time and life—so you can enjoy the time *of* your life!

But what happens to all that "saved" time? Can you store it for another day? No, but you can still spend it as you wish. You can allocate those extra hours to some of the activities you've dreamed about but never got around to doing.

Remember, if you don't use your time, you lose it. So find your purpose and live your dreams.

Start Living Your Purpose

You generally discover your purpose just by doing what you love to do. If you like writing or singing or tinkering with cars, then a career or hobby in that field is probably worth looking into. But when you feel unsure about your vocation and find yourself unmotivated and often frustrated, you are out of sync with your purpose in life.

Jill felt like that when she found a promising job after college. She studied journalism and music and ended up at a radio advertising agency—filing papers. As she watched the clock each day until morning coffee break, lunch hour, afternoon coffee, and quitting time, she wondered what was wrong with her. But when she taught piano lessons for three hours on Tuesday nights, the time with her students flew by and became the highlight of her week.

After nine months, it dawned on Jill that she loved teaching. So she went back to school to get her teaching credential in music. When she became a teacher, her creativity blossomed and she found her life purpose to teach and encourage students.

Where Do I Begin Finding My Purpose?

A series of steps can reveal your purpose, beginning with asking some important questions:

1. What part of my life do I enjoy the most? _____

2. What is it that I do that other people appreciate? _____

3. What don't I like to do? _____

4. What would I do if I didn't get paid to do it? _____

5. What would be the highest compliment I could receive from someone?
_____

Your answers to these questions will lead you to activities that you're made for as you look for the common threads. Move in the direction of your passion, and leave behind the situations or jobs that drain you.

Start Living Your Dreams

Goals usually spring from dreams. But don't just have pipe dreams about an unknown future; think about what you want to accomplish this month, this year, and three to five years from now.

If a goal is a dream with a date attached, which is the hard part for you: the dream or the date? If the dream is the hard part, brainstorm a dozen things you'd like to do: plan a trip to Hawaii, simplify your hectic schedule, or read a good book. Or your dream could be to win a tennis tournament, take a trip with interesting people, have your work appreciated, or receive a raise. Attach your dreams to dates each quarter of the year. Soon a real plan will unfold.

Intrinsic dreams depend on you and your performance. For example, you'd like to run a marathon or you've dreamed of acquiring a college degree.

Extrinsic goals depend on someone outside rewarding you or helping you succeed. These are more challenging to control but still worth picturing. For example, you envision yourself becoming the manager of your department at the office or receiving an award for your volunteer work at a local hospital.

> **Time-Saving Tip #99**
>
> Write your purpose statement for this phase of your life. Then frame it and read it daily. Example: "My purpose is to entertain and touch people through my teaching and singing."

To balance your life, consider creating some of each—goals you can initiate and carry out on your own and goals you would love to achieve that require the cooperation of others.

Where Do I Begin Finding My Dreams?

Put your dreams in writing with a positive statement. Following is an example that I wrote on my name tag at a writer's conference: "Today I am writing and marketing my book *Simplify Your Life: Get Organized and Stay That Way* with my dream team to change lives and influence people."

Time-Saving Tip #100

Once you write a dream down, relax and let your mind go to work to achieve it.

I put that sticker in my eyeglass case and read it every day for six months, each time I put on my glasses and took them off. The statement caught my attention and riveted me back to my goal. And my first book exceeded all expectations. That's when I learned the power of a dream written down and read daily.

To start living your dreams, you could write statements in a picture frame or shorten them for the top of your monthly calendar. If you need help with the wording, use the examples below:

- I am working out three times a week and changing my look from "flab" to "fab"!
- I found the ideal family room furniture (and at a bargain price) so we can host a big Super Bowl party this year.
- I'm solving problems at work and using my weekly "free choice" time to enjoy my favorite hobby.

It may sound a little contrived at first, but soon your statements will fall in line with your real life. And your mind will go to work to realize them. It really works!

Start Living—Today!

When you engage fully in each day, you really start living: purposeful in activities, attentive to people, and walking into your future with your eyes wide open. When you simplify your routines, you will have more time to do the things you want to do.

Here are two important questions to answer:

1. When do I feel most alive in my week, what am I doing, where am I, and who am I with? _____

2. Is there anything I'd rather be doing, or is this as good as it gets?

_____

This *Is* the Time of Your Life

Begin living today by starting with a dream affecting something in your everyday life. Then dream for bigger things beyond your local sphere. Write your dream down. Tweak the wording. Read it often. And start envisioning yourself feeling fully alive in the midst of your dream.

As Joel Osteen says, "You have to change your thinking before you can change your living. It's important that you program your mind for success. That won't happen automatically. Each day, you must *choose* to live with an attitude that expects good things to happen to you."

Once you expand your thinking, you can change your life by changing your time. Simplify the time you spend on routines and multiply the time you spend with people. Divide your free time between yourself and others, while subtracting the less important tasks to accomplish more. Today is the day to do the things you need and want to do.

> **Time-Saving Tip #101**
>
> Write your goals at the top of your calendar and read them every day to begin making them your reality very soon.

I close with the words of Ralph Waldo Emerson: "One of the illusions of life is that the present hour is not the critical, decisive hour. Write it on your heart that *every* day is the best day of the year."

This is your time. Live the moments, the days, and the months well, and you will accumulate a lifetime of satisfying memories and accomplishments. How you spend your time *is* your life. Live it well by choice, *your* choice, for that is what simplifying time is—your choice to stop running and *really* start living!

It's Your Time
Start Living—Today!

☐ Life is made up of "have-tos" and "want-tos." Choose to complete some of each every day.

☐ Keep growing and you'll improve day after day, year after year.

☐ Be an original. The more you are yourself, the less you are like others.

It is only possible to live happily ever after
on a day-to-day basis.

—Margaret Bonnano

Time Management Resources

RECOMMENDED BOOKS

Allen, David. *Getting Things Done.* New York: Viking, 2001.

Aslett, *Don. Clutter's Last Stand.* Cincinnati: Writer's Digest Books, 1984.

Canfield, Jack, Mark Victor Hansen, and Les Hewitt. *The Power of Focus.* Deerfield Beach, FL: Health Communications, 2000.

Covey, Stephen. *Seven Habits of Highly Effective People.* New York: Simon & Schuster, 1990.

Culp, Stephanie. *You Can Find More Time for Yourself Every Day.* Central Islip, NY: Betterway Books, 1994.

Decker, Dru Scott. *Finding More Time in Your Life.* Eugene, OR: Harvest House, 2001.

De Lonzor, Diana. *Never Be Late Again.* San Francisco: Post Madison Publishing, 2003.

Empson, Lila. *Simple Living for Busy People.* Grand Rapids: Inspirio, 2004.

Felton, Sandra. *The Messies Manual.* Grand Rapids: Revell, 2000.

Hemphill, Barbara. *Taming the Paper Tiger.* Washington, DC: Kiplinger, 1989.

Jones, Laurie Beth. *The Path: Creating Your Mission Statement for Work and for Life.* New York: Hyperion, 1998.

Knight, Porter. *Organized to Last.* Shoreham, VT: Discover Writing Press, 2005.

Lakein, Alan. *How to Get Control of Your Time and Life.* New York: Signet, 1973.

Mackenzie, Alec. *The Time Trap.* New York: MJF Books, 1997.

Maxwell, John. *Today Matters.* New York: Warner Faith, 2004.

McGraw, Phillip. *Life Strategies*. New York: Hyperion, 1999.

Morgenstern, Julie. *Never Check E-mail in the Morning*. New York: Simon & Schuster, 2004.

———. *Time Management from the Inside Out*. New York: Henry Holt, 2000.

Peel, Kathy. *The Family Manager Takes Charge*. New York: Perigee, 2003.

Ramsland, Marcia. *Simplify Your Life: Get Organized and Stay That Way*. Nashville: W Publishing Group, 2003.

Richardson, Cheryl. *Stand Up for Your Life*. New York: Free Press, 2002.

Schlenger, Sunny, and Roberta Roesch. *How to Be Organized in Spite of Yourself*. New York: New American Library, 1989.

Sher, Barbara. Wishcraft: *How to Get What you Really Want*. New York: Ballantine Books, 1979.

Smallin, Donna. *Organizing Plain and Simple*. Markham, Ontario: Storey, 2002.

Sprinkles, Patricia. *Women Who Do Too Much*. Grand Rapids: Zondervan, 2002.

Stack, Laura. *Leave the Office Earlier*. New York: Broadway, 2004.

Swenson, Richard A. *Margin*. Colorado Springs: NavPress, 1992.

Taylor, Harold. *Making Time Work for You*. Newmarket, Onatario: Harold Taylor Time Consultants, 1998.

The Women of Faith Daily Devotional. Plano, TX: Women of Faith, 2002.

Tullier, Michelle. *The Idiot's Guide to Overcoming Procrastination*. New York: Alpha, 1999.

RELATED WEB SITES

Dayrunner (www.dayrunner.com)

Daytimer (www.daytimer.com)

Kinkos (www.kinkos.com)

National Association of Professional Organizers (www.napo.net)

Office Depot (www.officedepot.com)

Office Max (www.officemax.com)

Staples (www.staples.com)

About the Author

Marcia Ramsland is well known as "The Organizing Pro" for her practical skills and tips to manage busy lives. She is an international speaker, author, and professional organizer who appears on radio and TV and in national magazines such as *Woman's Day* and *Better Homes and Gardens.* She has helped thousands of clients and audience participants conquer organizing issues. She and her husband live in San Diego and have three young adult children.

Marcia believes anyone can become more organized with the right teaching and tools. Her website, www.OrganizingPro.com — "The Place to Go to Simplify Your Everyday Life!" is a regular inspiration to those around the world. Visit it often for free tips and articles.

To contact Marcia for speaking or her ezine [Simplify Life], you may reach her at:

Marcia Ramsland, The Organizing Pro
Life Management Skills
P.O. Box 721792
San Diego, CA 92129
E-mail: Simplify@OrganizingPro.com
www.OrganizingPro.com

Other Books by Marcia Ramsland

Ages and Stages of Getting Children Organized. San Diego: RB Printing, 1998.

Simplify Your Life: Get Organized and Stay that Way! Nashville: W Publishing Group, 2003.

Simplify Your Space: Create Order and Reduce Stress! Nashville: W Publishing Group, 2007.

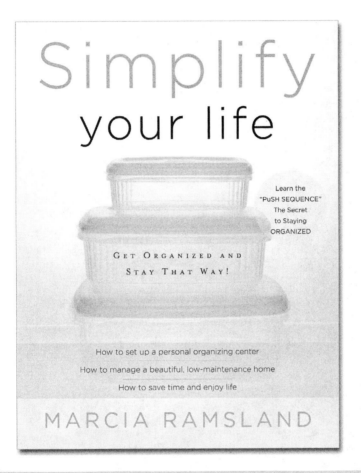

WOMEN OF FAITH

Amazing Freedom
2007

"So if the Son makes you free, you will be truly free." – John 8:36

We often catch *GLIMPSES OF FREEDOM* but what about the *promise* of being truly free? That's *AMAZING!* Women of Faith...as always, *FRESH, FABULOUS,* and *FUN-LOVING!*

2007 Conference Schedule*

March 15 - 17 San Antonio, TX The Alamodome	June 15 - 16 St. Louis, MO Savvis Center	August 10 - 11 Atlanta, GA Philips Arena	October 5 - 6 San Jose, CA HP Pavilion
April 13 - 14 Little Rock, AR ALLTEL Arena	June 22 - 23 Cleveland, OH Quicken Loans Arena	August 17 - 18 Calgary, AB Pengrowth Saddledome	October 12 - 13 Portland, OR Rose Garden Arena
April 20 - 21 Des Moines, IA Wells Fargo Arena	June 29 - 30 Seattle, WA KeyArena	August 24 - 25 Dallas, TX American Airlines Center	October 19 - 20 St. Paul, MN Xcel Energy Center
April 27 - 28 Columbus, OH Nationwide Arena	July 13 - 14 Washington, DC Verizon Center	September 7 - 8 Anaheim, CA Arrowhead Pond	October 26 - 27 Charlotte, NC Charlotte Bobcats Arena
May 18 - 19 Billings, MT MetraPark	July 20 - 21 Chicago, IL United Center	September 14 - 15 Philadelphia, PA Wachovia Center	November 2 - 3 Oklahoma City, OK Ford Center
June 1 - 2 Rochester, NY Blue Cross Arena	July 27 - 28 Boston, MA TD BankNorth Garden	September 21 - 22 Denver, CO Pepsi Center	November 9 - 10 Tampa, FL St. Pete Times Forum
June 8 - 9 Ft. Lauderdale, FL BankAtlantic Center	August 3 - 4 Ft. Wayne, IN War Memorial Coliseum	September 28 - 29 Houston, TX Toyota Center	November 16 - 17 Phoenix, AZ Glendale Arena

WOMEN OF FAITH
LI/E STYLE

Women of Faith's LifeStyle products offer practical resources designed to connect with and encourage women in everyday life. Focusing on realistic needs and current trends, each product selected fulfills the Women of Faith mission of nurturing women spiritually, emotionally, and relationally. Topics addressed include organization, decorating, entertaining, finance, and health.

WOMEN OF FAITH MISSION STATEMENT

Women of Faith wants all women to know God loves them unconditionally, no matter what. The ministry reaches out through motivational, yet moving conferences. Since 1996, more than 3,000,000 women have attended Women of Faith events in dozens of cities across North America.

Women of Faith is a nondenominational women's ministry committed to helping women of all faiths, backgrounds, age groups, and nationalities be set free to a lifestyle of God's grace. Founded specifically to meet the needs of women, Women of Faith is committed to nurturing women spiritually, emotionally, and relationally—whether it be in marriages, friendships, the workplace, or with their children. Our goal is to provide hope and encouragement in all areas of life, especially those that can wear women down and steal their joy and hope.

Women of Faith, which has become America's largest women's conference, exists to deliver great news to women: God loves them, and there are a bunch of girlfriends out there who love them too! Through laughter, music, dramas, and gut-level, real-life stories about how God has worked through the good and bad of our lives. Women of Faith reminds women that God is crazy about them!

For more information or to register for a conference, please visit *womenoffaith.com*